The Kung Fu of Grandmaster Chian Ho Yin

The Kung Fu of Grandmaster Chian Ho Yin

Exercise for the Bed-ridden and Scientific Ba Dwan Jin

Tai Chi Sword

Startling Rainbow Sword

This volume is a collection of three books authored by Grandmaster Chian Ho Yin.
Exercise for the Bed-ridden and Scientific Ba Dwan Jin (1958), *Tai Chi Sword* (1958), and *Startling Rainbow Sword* (1960).

Exercise for the Bed-ridden and Scientific Ba Dwan Jin was translated from the original Chinese by Mrs. Gir Lung Tuang Yin with assistance of Rina Lin.

Tai Chi Sword was translated from the original Chinese by Wen-Fen Chien (Wendy Mueckl) with assistance of her husband Jerry Mueckl.

Startling Rainbow Sword was translated from the original Chinese by Mrs. Gir Lung Tuang Yin with assistance of Rina Lin.

Research and editing by Jeffery Lee Nickel and A. F. Potter.
Typesetting and reproduction of pictures by A. F. Potter.
Additional photography by Jason Warwick.

ISBN-13: 978-0-692-32478-3
ISBN-10: 069232478X

Tai Chi Sword copyright © 1999 by the Chinese Kung Fu Center Inc.
This edition copyright © 2014 by the Chinese Kung Fu Center Inc.

All rights reserved. No part of this publication may be reproduced, stored in a retrieval system, or transmitted, in any form or by any means, electronic, mechanical, photocopying, recording, or otherwise, without prior written permission from the Chinese Kung Fu Center.

Chinese Kung-Fu Center
2120 West Clybourn Street
Milwaukee, WI 53233
(414) 933-7355

Disclaimer:

While every effort was made to ensure and verify accuracy in content, the author, publisher, and printer of this book make no representation or warranties with respect to the accuracy or completeness of the contents of this book or other materials included herein, and specifically disclaim any implied warranties of merchantability or fitness for any particular purpose, and are not liable for any damages resulting from the use of this book.

The contemporary photographs, featuring Jeffery Lee Nickel, are taken from various angles that allowed the photographer to capture all aspects of the posture. These photographs have been labeled to avoid any confusion in direction. In addition, these photographs represent the evolution of the forms over several decades, as taught by Grandmaster Yin.

This English Translation is Respectfully Dedicated to the Memory of

Grandmaster Chian Ho Yin

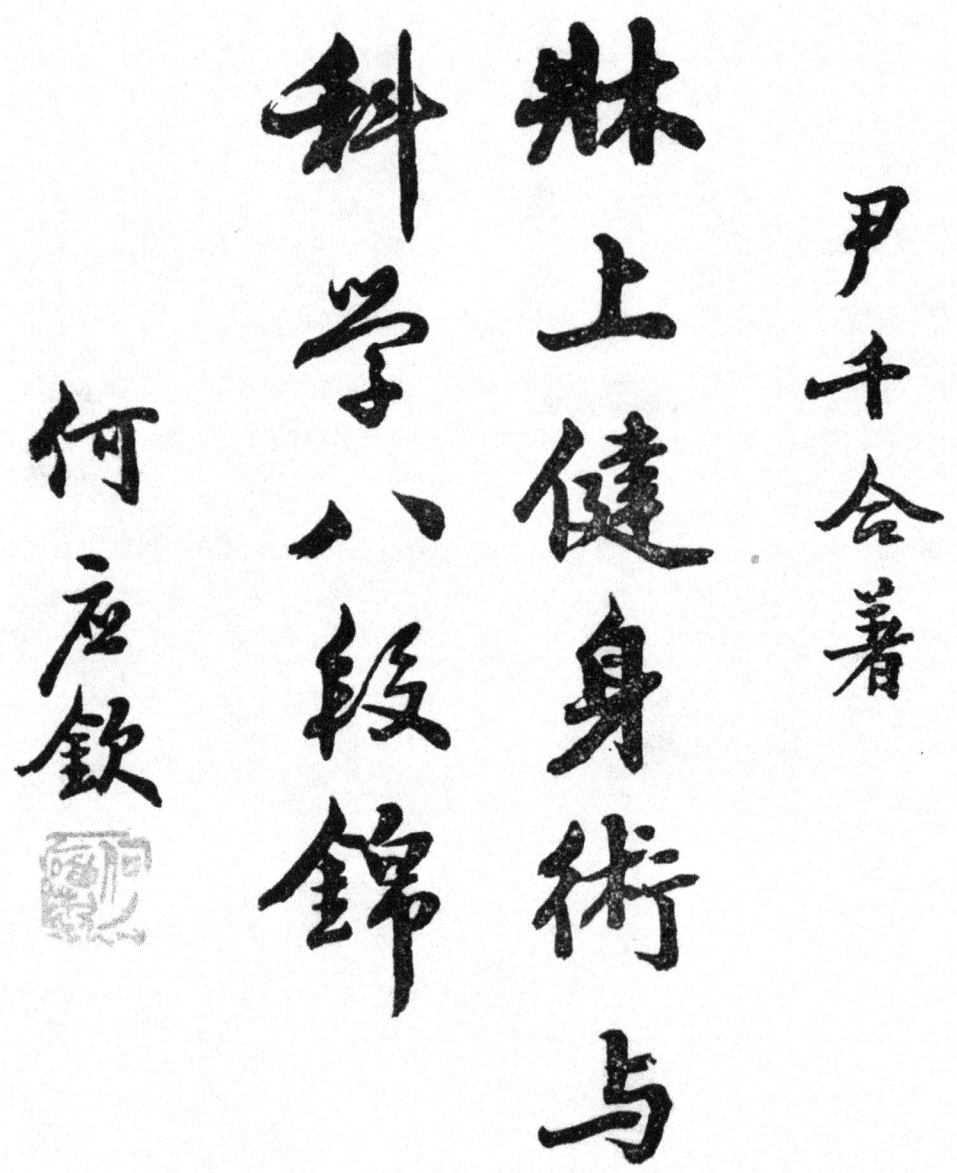

Exercise for the Bed-ridden and Scientific Ba Dwan Jin, (Original cover).
Calligraphy by General Ho Ying-Chin.

Tai Chi Sword, (Original cover).
Calligraphy by General Ho Ying-Chin.

國術叢書之九

驚虹劍術

尹千合自署

Startling Rainbow Sword, (Original cover).
Calligraphy by Grandmaster Chian Ho Yin.

牀上健身術與科學八段錦

（附自我電療攝生術八段）

"Exercise for the Bed-ridden and Scientific Ba Dwan Jin."
Calligraphy by General Ho Ying-Chin.

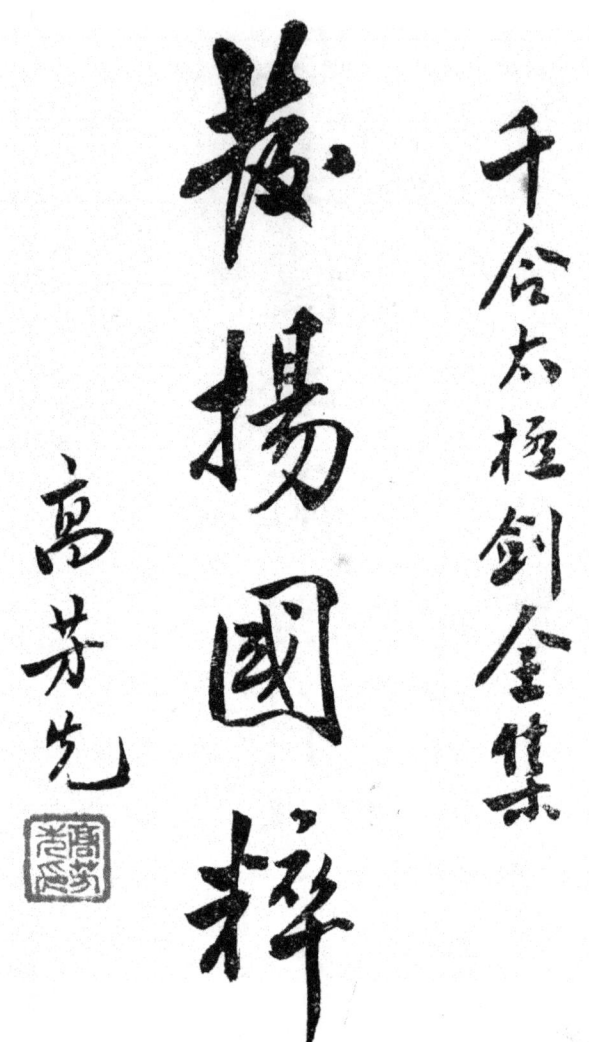

"Yin Chian Ho's Tai Chi Sword,
Developing and Spreading the Best of the Country."
Calligraphy by Kao Fang Hsien.

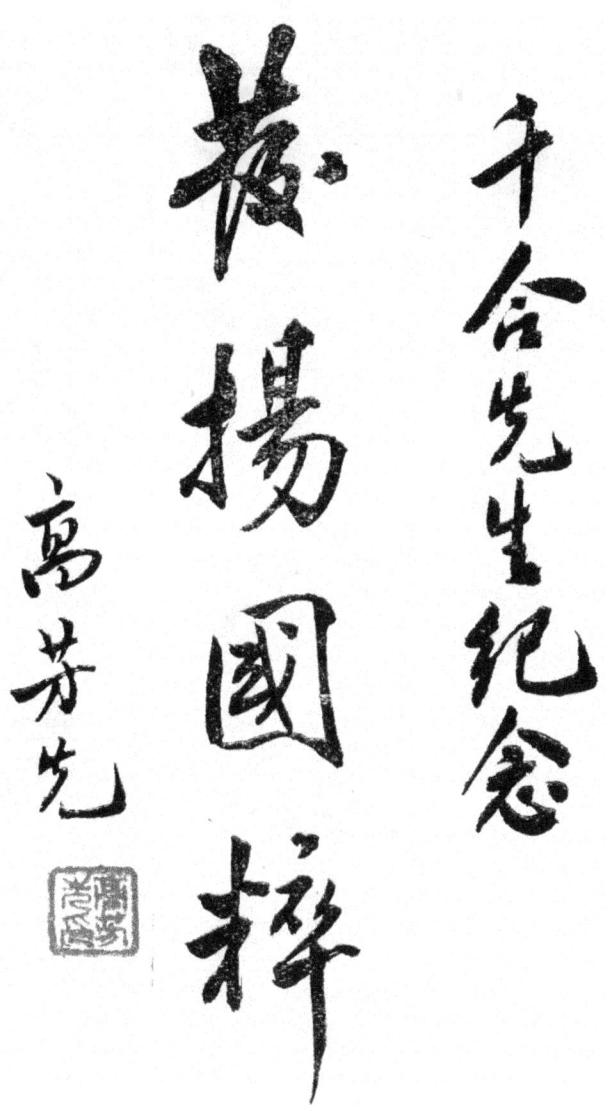

"A precious offering by which to remember Yin Chian Ho,
Developing and Spreading the Best of the Country."
Calligraphy by Kao Fang Hsien.

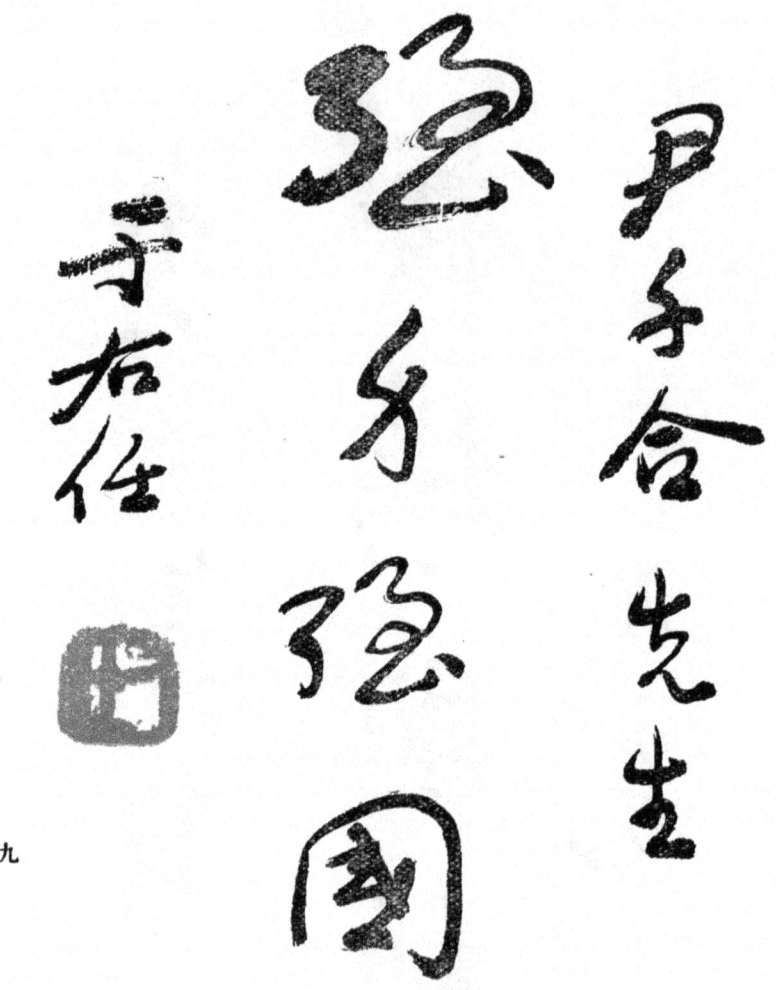

**"Strong body, strong country."
Calligraphy by Ee Yo Lin.**

Mr. Lin, a famous calligrapher, came to Taiwan with Chiang Kai Shek after the Chinese revolution. He knew that he could never return; therefore, he asked that he be buried on the highest mountain in Taiwan so that he could watch over China for all of time.

千合先生國術叢書出刊紀念

鍛鍊身心
砥勵志節

王一之 敬題

"Train the body and spirit; and virtue,
Self esteem and morals become strong."
Calligraphy by Hong E Chi.

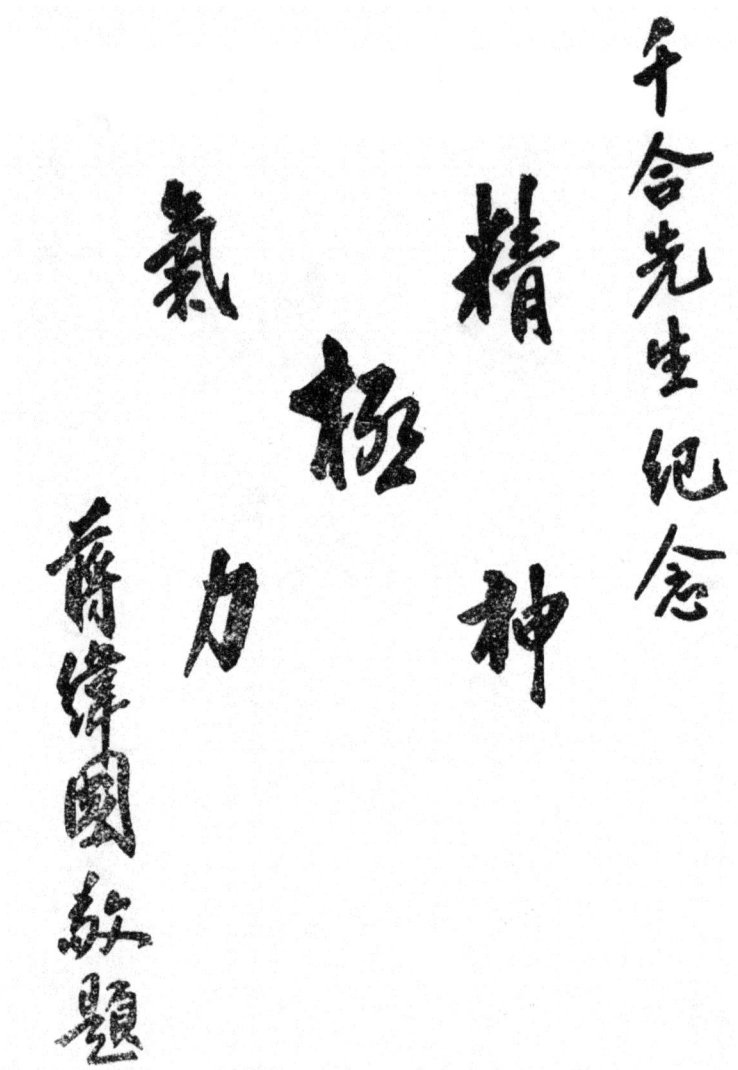

"Spirit, Ultimate, Energy."
Calligraphy by Chiang Wei-Kuo.
Second son of Chiang Kai-Shek.

Table of Contents

About the Book i
Preface 1 iii
Preface 2 v
Preface 3 vi
1: Introduction to Chinese Martial Arts 1
2: Criticism of Chinese Kung Fu 3
3: The Attitudes and Morals Required 4
4: The "Needs" of Kung Fu Practice 6
5: Cautions of Martial Arts Training 7
6: Introduction to Ba Dwan Jin Exercise 8
7: Common Sense Preparation for Ba Dwan Jin Practice 9
8: Key Benefits from Ba Dwan Jin Practice 10
9: Lying Ba Dwan Jin 11
10: Continuous Ba Dwan Jin 21
11: Sitting Ba Dwan Jin (The Generation of Your own Chi) 32
12: General Introduction to Sword Skill 42
13: Explanation of Sword Skill Techniques and Their Functions 43
14: Introduction to Tai Chi Sword 45
15: Hints for the Practice of Tai Chi Sword 47
16: Order and Names of Each Posture of Tai Chi Sword 48
17: Foot Step and Directional Figures 51
18: Tai Chi Sword 57
19: Order and Names of Each Posture of Startling Rainbow Sword 178
20: Startling Rainbow Sword 181

ABOUT THE BOOK

By Jeffery Lee Nickel

In order to fully appreciate the historical and martial significance of this book, we need to address the various personal endorsements, that in Taiwan (ROC), during the 1950's, was indeed monumental.

The original book cover, which we have reproduced, contains the endorsement and calligraphy of Nationalist China's most recognizable hero, General Ho Ying-Chin. General Ho's career included Commander of Nationalist Main Force-I Corps (1925), Military Governor Fukien Province (1926), War Minister (1928), the Ho-Umezu Agreement with Japan (1935), Army Chief of Staff (1945), as well as presiding over the Japanese surrender in September of 1945.

Preface #1 was written by Shen Hung Lieh. In March, 1938, Admiral Shen became Governor of Shantung Province in Northern China, as well as being responsible for the military administration headquarters in Qing Dow, Shantung Province.

Included in the first preface is a reference to Kao Fang Hsien and Yang Ching Shen. Both were generals who headed a team of martial art instructors in the army. General Kao's Shaolin was recognized as "swift and authoritative," he also excelled at Shuai Chiao.

Preface #2 was written by Chen Pan Ling (1890-1967). Chen's father studied at the Shaolin Temple in Honan Province and provided his son with many excellent teachers. In addition, Chen furthered his studies by learning Tai Chi Chuan at the famed Honan village of Chen Chia Kou. During World War II, Chen was appointed Deputy Chief of the Central Boxing Association at Chungking. After leaving for Taiwan, Chen became the president of Taichung College and head of the Chinese Boxing Association in Taiwan (1949-1967).

Preface #3 was written by Yin Chian Ho (1903-1988). Master Yin, who authored this book, makes references to Chen Pan Ling, Ahn Ding Bang, and Wang Shu Chin. Little is known about Master Ahn other than that he studied the original Wu's Style Tai Chi

Chuan from Wu Chian Chuan, and that he taught at the Peking University (Gymnasium) of Sports and Recreation.

Wang Shu Chin (1904-1981) was a 230 pound expert in Tai Chi Chuan, Hsing I and Pa Kua. He studied, in China, with Chang Chao Tung (recognized as one of China's greatest masters) from 1929-1938. As a testimony to his strength and skill, Master Wang allowed anyone to strike him in the stomach or kick him in the knee, calf or ankle, always with the same result, no pain, no movement, nothing.

I hope that by reading and studying this book one would not only appreciate the historical and martial significance, but take it a step further and internalize the higher aspects of Chinese Martial Arts, such as proper attitudes and morals (Chapter 3). Far too often, in the pursuit of profit, students are taught only to fight and be aggressive. This is not the legacy of the Chinese Martial Arts, nor should it be. Health, integrity, and self-defense are the realm of the true master.

(2014) This new addition brings together three of Grandmaster Yin's Kung Fu treasures in one volume. This new volume includes Master Yin's *Exercise for the Bedridden and Scientific Ba Dwan Jin*, *Tai Chi Sword*, and *Startling Rainbow Sword*. The Tai Chi Sword and Startling Rainbow Sword sections have been reproduced to include contemporary pictures that reflect the final evolution of those respective styles. By including both sets of pictures we have tried to retain the spirit of the original and provide our students with a valuable reference for the contemporary form.

PREFACE 1

By Shen Hung Lieh

A healthy body is the prerequisite of having a vigorous spirit, knowledge and career. If you desire to establish and benefit yourself, as well as others, you must first put your emphasis on physical education. Practice every day and persist until the end. This is what we call strengthening one's self. The prosperity of a country and the level of its culture are determined by the strength of all the people. If you desire to develop a higher culture and make your country prosperous, you need to spread physical education from small groups to society, from the cities to the villages. This is to plant strong seeds.

There are varieties of physical education, such as track and sports, which are very popular in the world and in our country. But according to our custom and environment, practicing the martial arts does not need equipment, is not limited by time and place, and has no cost. It is much easier to develop and spread in our present situation. Martial arts emphasize three pairs of one; heart and intention are one, intention and chi are one, and chi and strength are one. Martial arts make your heart stable, your focus concentrated, brings one closer to the truth, and causes one to uphold and admire morality, including public service, the love of righteousness, and the support of, and aid to, those in danger. In addition to strengthening your own body, and planting a strong seed, martial arts can also protect your home town and country.

During the period that the Japanese invaded China, I was responsible for the military administration in Qing Dow, Shantung province. Because of the difficult situation, we promoted martial arts as our strategy. Sixty thousand citizens were trained in martial arts along with the military, to stand against the enemy. In the battle of July seventh [1937], we were able to defeat the Japanese and complete our mission, due to the contribution of a team of martial arts instructors led by Kao Fang Hsien and Yang Ching Shen. As an instructor, Mr. Yin Chian Ho trained hundreds of our soldiers and led them into battle against Japan. Martial arts was successfully used to protect our country from the invaders. As a result, people believe that martial arts can be used to protect their country.

After the Communists took over mainland China [in 1949], these three leaders followed the military order to move to Taiwan. After their military assignment, they continued to teach martial arts for many years, Mr. Yin also served in the field of education. Many people followed his teaching [of Chinese martial arts]. After school hours, he wrote Tai Chi Sword and Ba Dwan Jin. When the books were finished, he asked me to write the preface, because of my love for martial arts. Even though I don't have a lot of insight about them, at close to eighty years of age, I am old but not weak. So I believe I have obtained the benefit of practicing the martial arts. Now this is a scientific age. If we want to be among those powerful countries, we need much more research along with a strong cultural basis. To improve people's health, we cannot ignore the spreading of the martial arts. Mr. Yin continually strengthens himself, while at the same time planting the seeds to protect the country. This is why he wrote these books. His work is a great help to the spreading of the martial arts.

PREFACE 2

By Chen Pan Ling

Chinese martial arts are our essential culture. They are a unique skill. By following this way, countries were enriched and soldiers strengthened throughout our history. The theory is very deep, and the skills developed are marvelous. The Chinese martial arts are superior to the martial arts of all other countries. From a corporate viewpoint, they can produce a strong seed and protect a country. From an individual viewpoint, they can prolong life. In the recent ten years (1950s), more people have begun to favor western sports. This has prevented the further development of the martial arts which were inherited from our ancestors over thousands of years. That is why our race is so weak. This is very sad.

The way of the sword is the highest skill in our history. Since this skill emphasizes individual practice, almost no book has been written on this subject. Later learners are left with no reference. All they can do is grope like blind men. So, the best part of the sword skill is lost. Mr. Yin is both very scholarly and very skillful in martial arts. His research is endless, and he is willing to share what he has learned from his research, writing systematically in order to spread the martial arts. The contents of his recent books, Tai Chi Sword, Exercise for the Bed-ridden, and Scientific Ba Dwan Jin, are very rich, the theory very clear, and the procedures are detailed. They are a great contribution to Chinese Martial Arts. All my life, I have promoted martial arts. After coming to Taiwan, I still have the desire to freely educate the people and improve their health, with the purpose of rescuing our country and strengthening the seed. The intention of Mr. Yin's book is the same as my will. So I am very happy to write this preface.

PREFACE 3

By Yin Chian Ho

My knowledge is shallow and my skill is dull. How can I have the courage to write this book and let people laugh at me? Only because I myself have deeply benefited from Chinese martial arts, and therefore wouldn't dare to be selfish. I desire to introduce this to all the people, especially those who are physically weak. Diligent practice will make a weak person strong. I have written this book out of self respect and love for others, so that I could inspire others to follow.

In my childhood, I was often sick. Even at twenty years old I was still very weak. No medicine could help me. My parents were very worried. We had a neighbor named Fu Ting Jia. He was skillful in martial arts, so I asked him to teach me. As a result, my stubborn sickness was cured, and my desire to learn more was increased. At that time, a very famous Tai Chi Chuan teacher by the name of Ahn Ding Bang was serving at a gymnasium in Peking. I packed up all my things and traveled there to learn from him. Master Ahn's skill was most excellent, and he taught tirelessly. I practiced diligently day and night. Fortunately, I caught the vision! My strength became full, and I became a different person than I was before.

During the war with Japan, I followed Chairman Shen Hung Lieh, serving in the military. Mr. Shen always promoted Chinese martial arts, so they designated me as a martial arts instructor in the army. I loved to do this, because this is my passion. The soldiers benefited greatly from martial arts during the war.

After the Communists occupied the mainland, I followed the government and moved to Taiwan, where I served in the field of education. Many young people who loved Chinese martial arts followed me to practice. So I had to be strong and continue my exercise. I received much advise from my mentor Chen Pan Ling, and also from the famous expert Wang Shu Chin. After teaching class, I used my time to do research in martial arts. Whether my research was in Shao Lin Kung Fu, Tai Chi, or the use of gun, knife, sword or staff, as long as it is healthy and can be applied to defense, I wrote about it in my books, which include Tai Chi Chuan, Tai Chi Sword, Exercise for the Bed-ridden, and Scientific Ba Dwan Jin, Twelve Pathway Tan Tui, and Tai Zu

Chang Chuan. I asked my good friend Lui Hwa Nung, to take pictures of each posture to put into the books. Because I am living in Taiwan, I am short of reference books. I have to rely heavily on my memory of what my teachers taught and my personal research. That is why there may be mistakes. I have only published Tai Chi Sword, Exercise for the Bed-ridden and Scientific Ba Dwan Jin, as they are not well known, and to provide my students with a reference. I deeply hope all martial arts experts will make up for any lack in these books. This will encourage me.

Grandmaster Yin outside his home, Milwaukee, 1980.

Chapter 1

Introduction to Chinese Martial Arts

Chinese martial arts are our essential culture. The theory behind them is very high and deep. The skills developed are marvelous, full of the spirit of loyalty, courage and righteousness. Through practice, the Chinese martial arts are able to make the stubborn flexible, the cowardly courageous, and to turn weakness into strength. The sports of every country in the world have their own advantages. However, according to our present situation, (post-war Taiwan) to save money, training facility space, and yet still enable everyone to practice, Chinese martial arts seem more convenient than other sports. President Chiang Kai Shek spoke concerning sports and entertainment: "Chinese martial arts are not only for defensive fighting, but also have much more significance in physical education. The highest realm of the martial arts is to make one calm and peaceful. Strength will follow the leading of the mind. Foreign sports cannot compare with this. That is why we call it Chinese martial arts." This quote is simple and to the point, yet adequate to alert us.

It doesn't matter whether the Chinese martial art is Shao-lin or Wu-Dong. As long as the Kung Fu is full of skill, strength will be present within gentleness, and gentleness will be present within strength. Changes cannot be detected but can be applied according to your desire. Later descendants have declared Shao-lin to be an external sect, and Wu-Dong an inward sect, and again subdivided both of these into Hua-mun and Hong-mun, Southern and Northern sects. Each have their own opinions. Each selfishly feels they have the real thing, and have closed the door to the other, wanting to keep their secrets rather than passing them down, while at the same criticizing the other. There is no gain to themselves in this, and there is no benefit to the country. This is very sad.

We are now in the stage of fighting against Communism and Russia. All those in Chinese martial arts should tear down their walls and do research together with the same goal of advancing martial arts. On one hand, we will set up different levels of teaching material to train good instructors, and improve teaching methods. On the other hand, we hope to be able to spread martial arts from the military to the schools, and from the cities to the villages, especially emphasizing physical and psychological training, to create a realm of calm and peace, a realm of strength following the mind. We need to make martial arts scientific, popular, accepted by all, morally sound, and a good medicine to rescue the country and this age. Although I am not sharp, I am willing to hold the whip while following behind.

Chapter 2

Criticism of Chinese Kung Fu

- Some teachers may not share all of their knowledge. Eighty percent may be openly taught while twenty percent is selfishly kept secret. This only hurts the Kung Fu.

- As a student gains skills, they may bully those weaker. A good teacher must teach ethics and compassion.

- When two martial artists perform differently, they quickly become enemies. Differences will exist, but if the basics are strong then it is good Kung Fu.

- Some question the usefulness of Kung Fu in modern society. But if your spirit is strengthened, and your body grows strong, the benefit to society is great. Confidence grows as the body strengthens itself. With both these strong, even in miserable times, one can survive.

In Chinese Kung Fu there are two paths: Shaolin (external) and Wu Tang (internal). Shaolin is further divided into northern and southern styles. Japanese Judo and Korean Tai Kwan Do originate from Chinese martial arts. Japanese Karate (empty hand) and Tai Kwan Do (feet/leg work) have been taught throughout the world yet Chinese Kung Fu, which is the original seed, and comprises both hands and feet, has not yet been taught to its fullest capacity. Chinese martial art is at a loss if it does not address this issue.

Chapter 3

The Attitudes and Morals Required for Practicing Chinese Martial Arts

Substantiality: A person who practices Chinese martial arts must be substantial. A substantial person is simple and honest; he cannot be fidgety or proud. Confucius said that if a gentleman is not substantial, he cannot be respected, and what he has learned cannot be maintained.

Respectfulness: When you contact people, you have to have a heart that respects others. Those who respect others will also be respected in return. Your attitude must be humble, respectful and honest. Do not flatter others.

Peacefulness: To practice Chinese martial arts one must be calm and peaceful. One cannot be fierce in order to suppress others. Wild behavior is most shameful. When interacting with people or things, one must be peaceful.

Generosity: A person who practices Chinese martial arts has to be unselfish and without prejudice. In handling his affairs, he must be generous, unselfish, open and sincere, having an uncompromising spirit.

Diligence: A person who practices Chinese martial arts has to be diligent. He cannot be lazy. If you practice diligently, your Kung Fu will naturally be deep.

Righteousness: A person who practices Chinese martial arts has to be righteous. You do what you should do, and you don't do what you shouldn't do. If you know what is righteous and you don't do it, you are without courage.

Kindness: A person who practices Chinese martial arts has to be kind; both to people and to things. Have a kind heart and a spirit of love.

Loyalty: A person who practices Chinese martial arts cannot stir up fights for selfish gain. He should contribute his skill, body and heart to his country and his people.

The philosophy of Chinese Kung Fu is most important. It is essential to defend the weak and reject being a bully. Self defense for a purpose, not reckless attack. Those people at the highest level of Kung Fu have a peaceful spirit and are motivated towards cultivating high moral standards. Be kind to others and you will receive kindness in return.

Always emphasize self-defense, not fighting. If one bullies another because their skill is greater then they have obliterated the entire foundation on which Chinese Kung Fu is built. Strengthen your body and avoid the practice of "Dead Kung Fu," which is training that allows one to be struck.

In training, the spirit/heart is first, the body second. Therefore, if a student with a bad spirit appears (using their training for an evil purpose), it is the teacher's responsibility to teach them no more.

Chapter 4

The "Needs" of Kung Fu Practice

1. The learning of Kung Fu is a gradual process. If you learn quickly you will also forget quickly and your body will not have a chance to strengthen itself. Learning quickly will result in sore and strained muscles and you won't be able to endure long training sessions.

2. When training, train continuously and consistently. You must train almost every day. If you take several days off at a time your body will not receive the full benefit of Kung Fu.

3. Do not brag of your skills and training. Find peace of mind and extinguish arrogance or society will look down upon you no matter how skilled you may be.

4. Show respect to your teacher by having good relations with your Kung Fu brothers and sisters, and maintain high moral standards for yourself.

Chapter 5

Cautions of Martial Arts Training

1. Those that train should not drink. If you drink, do not drink to drunkenness, as your blood pressure will be compromised. Do not drink and train. Also do not train while in an angry mood, as your chi will be negative.

2. Don't train on an empty stomach or you will become hungry and your stomach can become damaged. Likewise, do not train on a full stomach as both extremes may cause stomach and intestinal tract problems.

3. Training can take place during all seasons. Rest 30 minutes before consuming a meal; this will allow your spirit to become calm. After eating, wait one hour before you begin to train, as your stomach needs to relax before you engage in activity. This is common sense; do not forget.

4. Wear baggy pants and supportive shoes when you train. Do not wear stiff leather shoes while you train.

5. Even in summer wear clothing. Training without clothes is not healthy.

6. Training in the morning is ideal, but do not train to the point of total exhaustion. As a beginner, you will experience soreness and fatigue after training. Do not worry; your strength will return after a short rest. This is the exchange of strength and chi. Therefore, continue training and don't be discouraged; your body will recover.

Chapter 6

Introduction to Ba Dwan Jin Exercise

I have written this book so that others may benefit from my love of kung fu. I have spent many years researching what makes a body strong and healthy, so that others may learn about themselves and be well.

Ba Dwan Jin translates to eight pieces of brocade. The term brocade refers to a beautiful, strong and precious weave of cloth and draws an analogy between this exercise, and a beautiful valuable material.

This book offers three styles of Ba Dwan Jin:

1. Lying on the floor
2. Standing
3. Seated

All three styles serve to strengthen the body, increase flexibility and ensure good blood and chi circulation. In addition, an internal cleansing occurs that will strengthen the immune system.

The exercises in this book are performed slowly and are practical for men and women regardless of age or physical condition. Anyone can participate and receive the benefits of these exercises. Each of the three exercises may be completed in 10 minutes and are easy to learn. The exercises are based on Tai Chi principles and utilize a person's own energy to strengthen the body and heal sickness. This approach to health it is an ancient Chinese concept that has been nearly forgotten and its use discontinued. These principles have enormous potential and will yield amazing results if practiced daily.

Chapter 7

Common Sense Preparation for Ba Dwan Jin Practice

No exercise will show its results in two or three sessions. Therefore discipline is needed in order to fully benefit from practice. Practice once in the morning and again in the evening. Prepare by drinking a cup of warm water with a little salt - this helps to prevent dehydration. Begin by softening your thoughts and focusing on the exercise; don't be concerned about the day's activity. If your health is poor pace yourself, no need to push yourself - move slowly. Look at the pictures and follow the form. For beginners, muscles and tendons will stretch and become sore, tolerate this and you will improve.

Chapter 8

Key Benefits from Ba Dwan Jin Practice

Although these exercises are easy to learn and practice, the benefits will allow a person to live a long and happy life. As you exercise your endurance will increase, as well as your bones and muscles becoming stronger. The body becomes healthy and beautiful. Internal circulation of blood and chi improve with the physical movement and breathing of the exercise. The gastrointestinal tract and overall appetite will also improve. Your outer appearance will change as your health and body are made stronger and you will be more alert.

Chapter 9

Lying Ba Dwan Jin

(Common Names, Explanation of Movement and Positional Figures)

Preparation

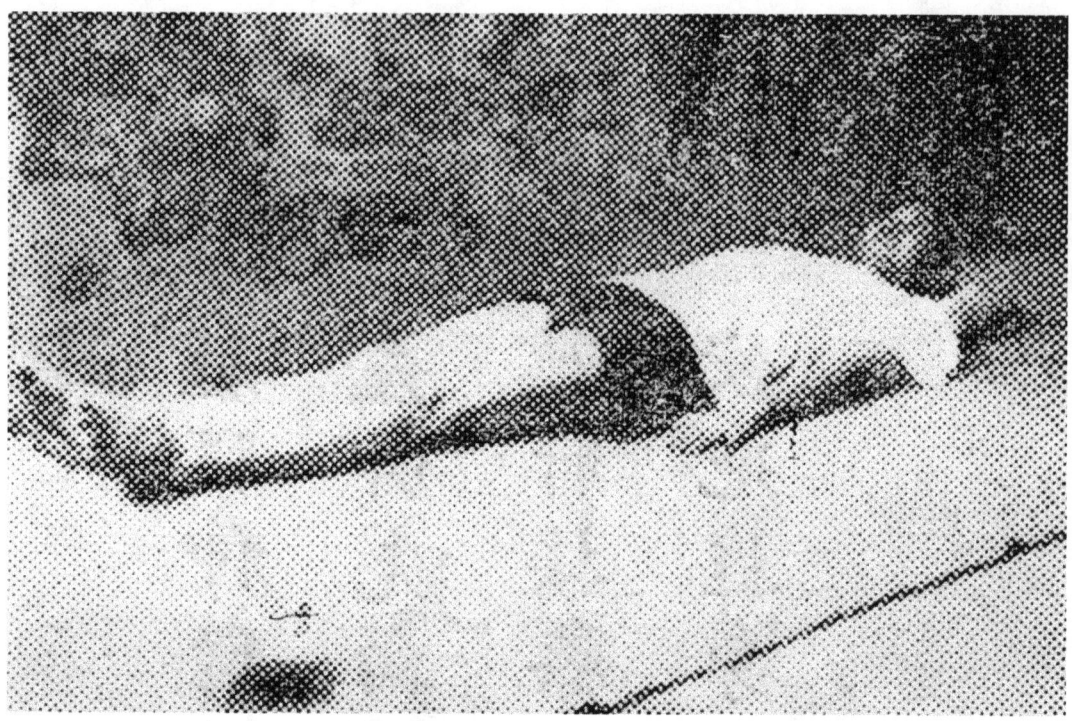

1. Lie on your back on a firm surface, hands at your side, palms down – calm your thoughts.

2. Raise hands and rub together until they are warm - this will increase blood flow and cause your body's energy to flow through your entire body.

3. With both hands massage the abdomen.

4. When finished, place hands back to beginning position.

1. *Flex Feet, Stretch Hands*

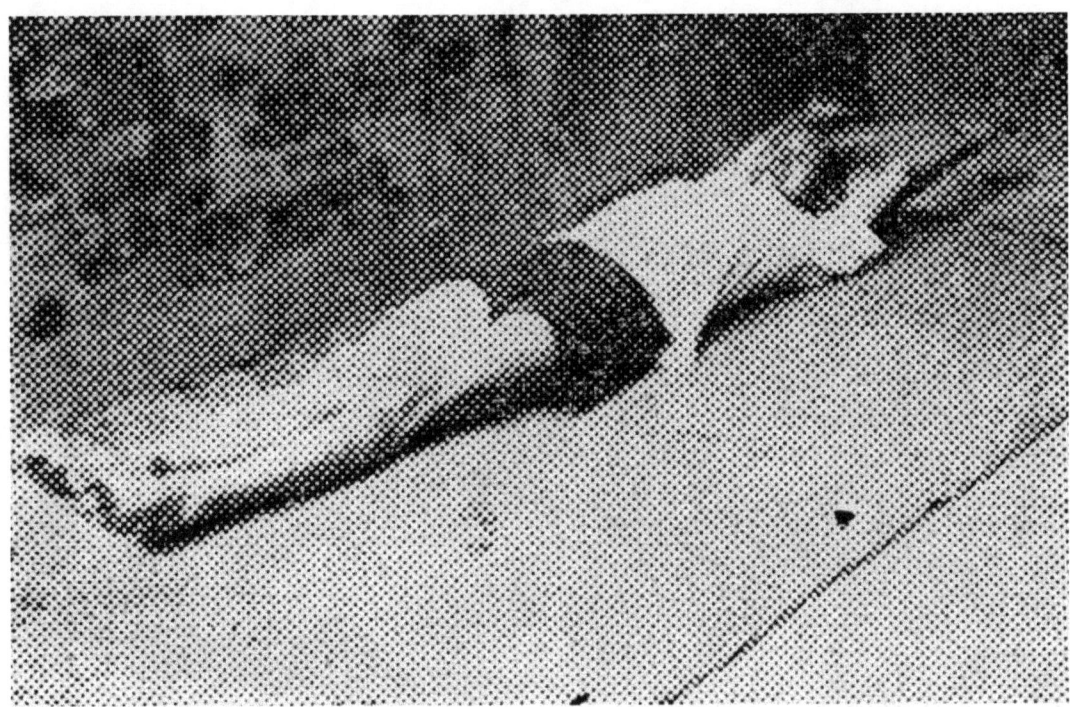

Explanation of Movement:

Lying with palms down, lengthen your body.

- Stretching the sinews/tendons promotes healthy blood flow.

- Strengthens the frame of the body, improves posture as well as the appearance of the figure.

- Helps to enhance coordination and reaction time.

Example: Humans do not stretch often but cats do. As a result, cats are coordinated, flexible and have quick reflexes.

2. *Holding Nape of Neck, Sitting, Tightening Abdomen (Sit-ups)*

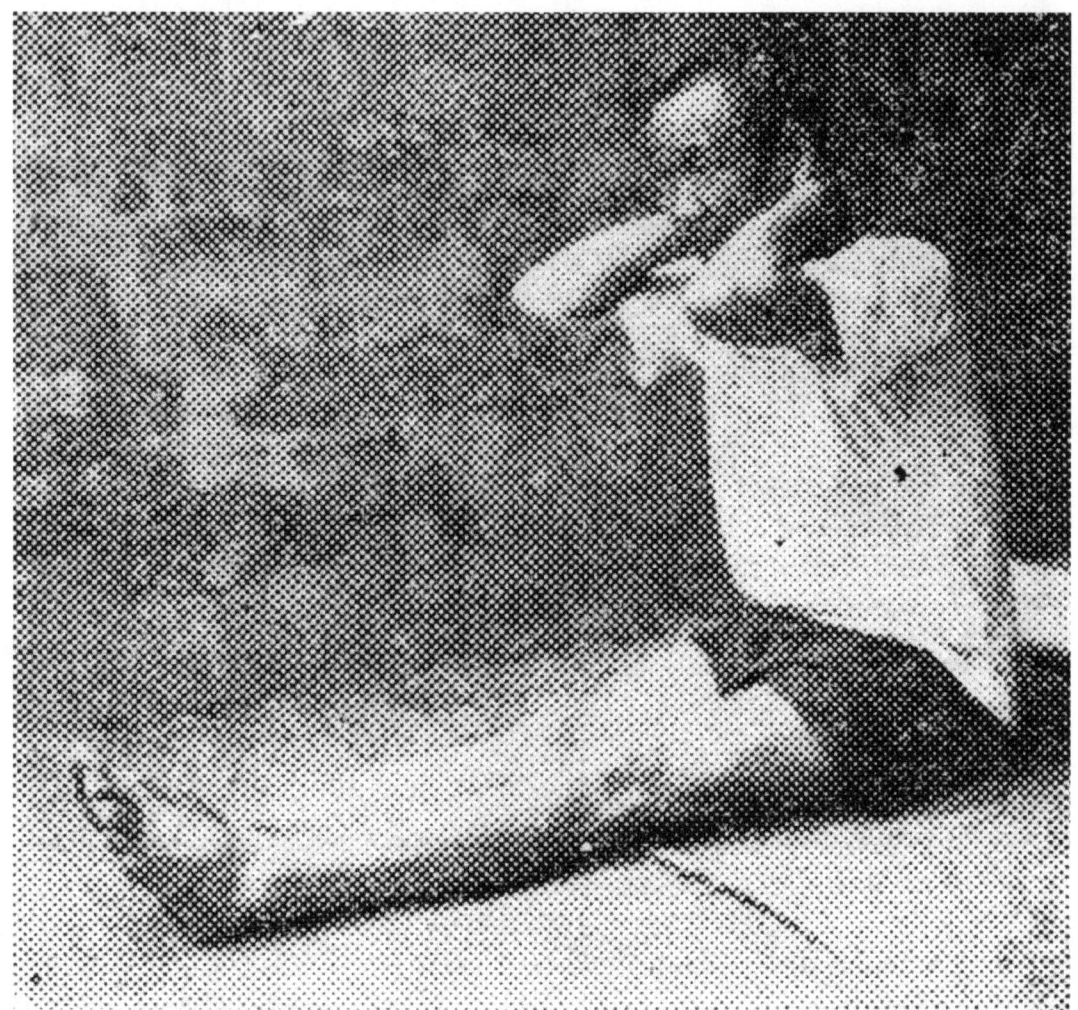

Explanation of Movement:

Keeping legs straight, tighten the abdomen to pull the torso up.

- Strengthens the waist and lower back.

- Tightening the abdomen forms a smaller waist.

3. *Right Elbow Touches Left Knee (Right Sided Crossover)*

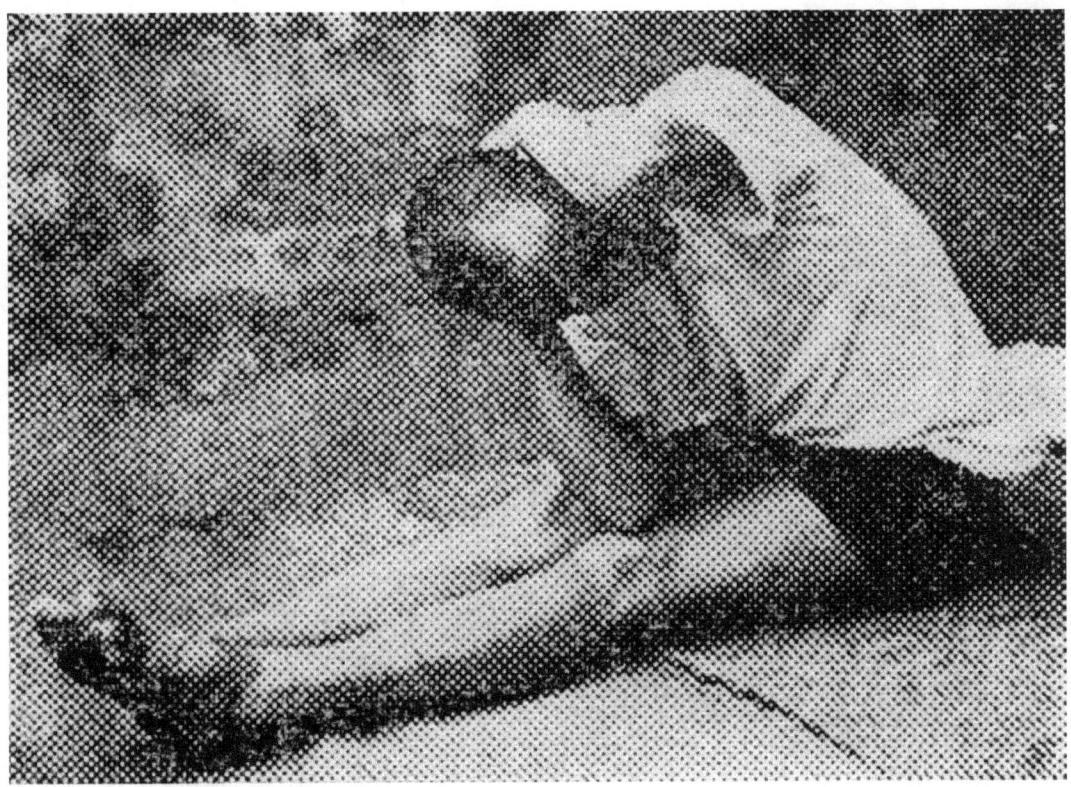

Explanation of Movement:

Refer to picture.

- Stretches and strengthens the neck, abdomen and ribs.

4. *Left Elbow Touches Right Knee (Left Sided Crossover)*

Explanation of Movement:

Refer to picture, same as exercise #3 but on the opposite side.

5. *Both Elbows Touch Knees*

Explanation of Movement:

Bending straight forward, touch elbows to knees

- When first practiced, tendons will ache due to stretching. Do not strain or overexert yourself.

- In the elderly especially, elbows may not be able to reach the knees, therefore don't press.

- Over time the muscles and tendons will strengthen and become more flexible.

- Practicing this regularly will eventually allow you to touch your elbows to your knees.

- Tightening ones abdomen stimulates the appetite.

6. *Palms of Hand to Flat of Foot*

Explanation of Movement:

Bend forward, place palm of hands over toes, on the flat of the foot.

- The arms and legs are equally/evenly extended, this improves flexibility.

- One's abdomen isn't "out" as much so, easily - the limbs may be equalized.

7. *Pushing Up*

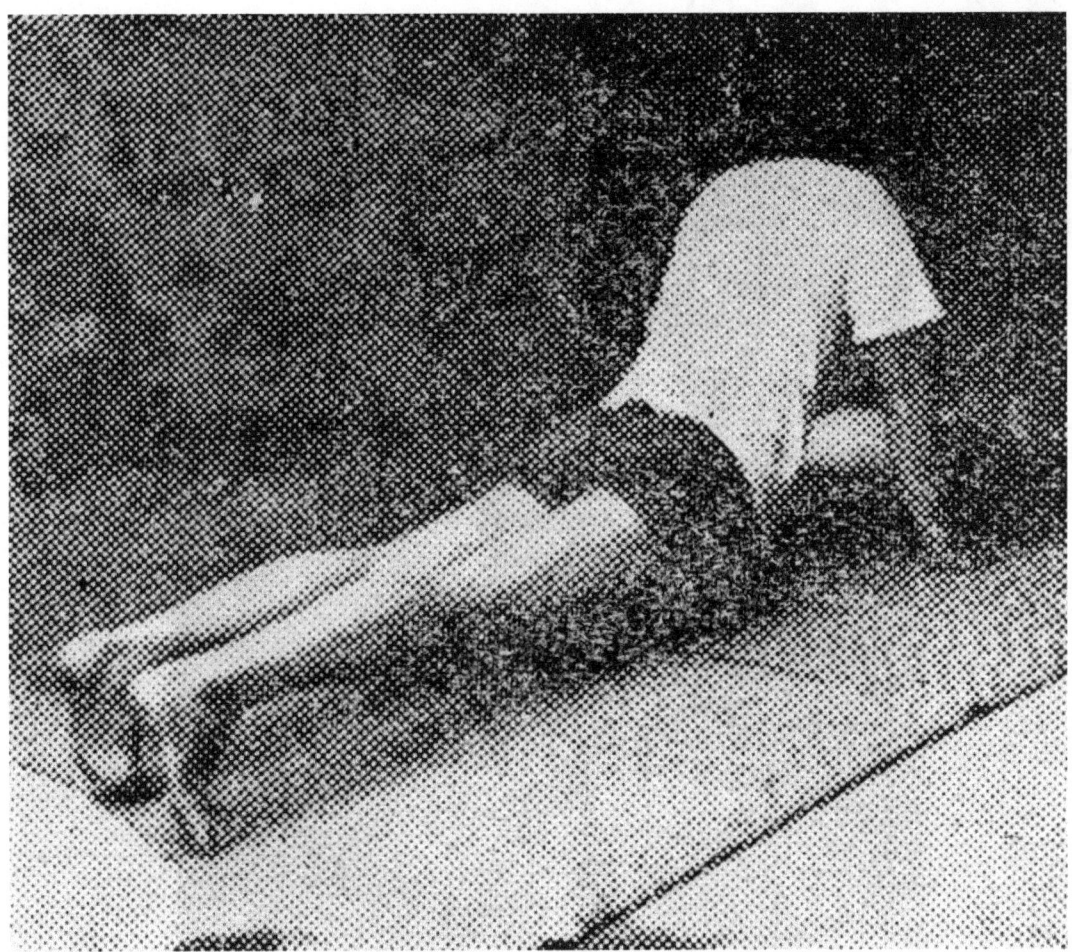

Explanation of Movement:

Push-up position, push yourself up evenly.

- Strengthens shoulders lower back, waist and legs.

8. *Sitting Quietly*

Explanation of Movement:

Common position of monks in meditation.

- Quiet the soul, collect chi in Dan Tien.
- Power to heal/deal with sickness is generated here.
- Deep breathing.
- Calming.

Chapter 10

Continuous Ba Dwan Jin

(Common Names, Explanation of Movement and Positional Figures)

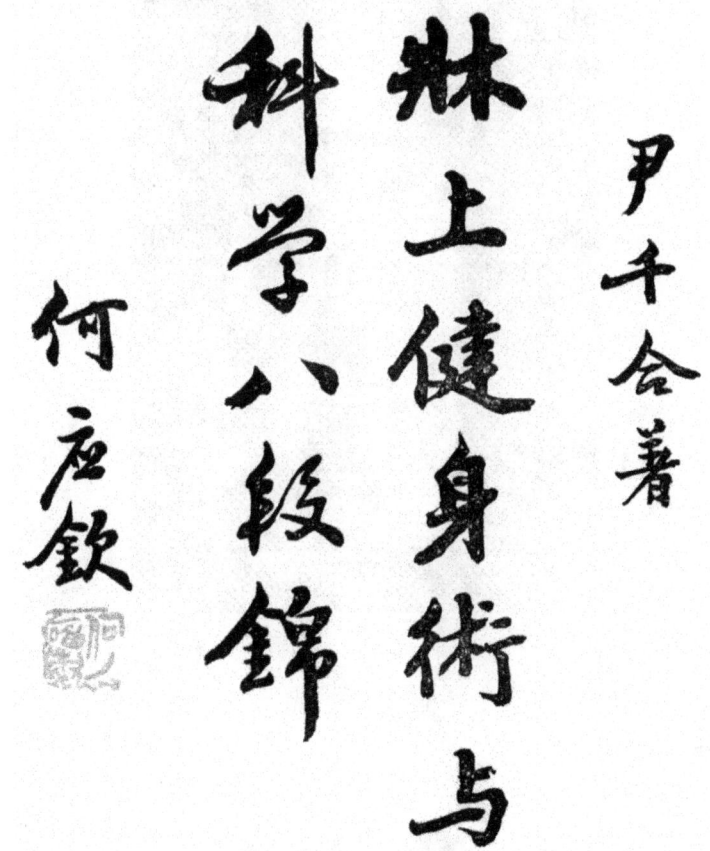

Preparation

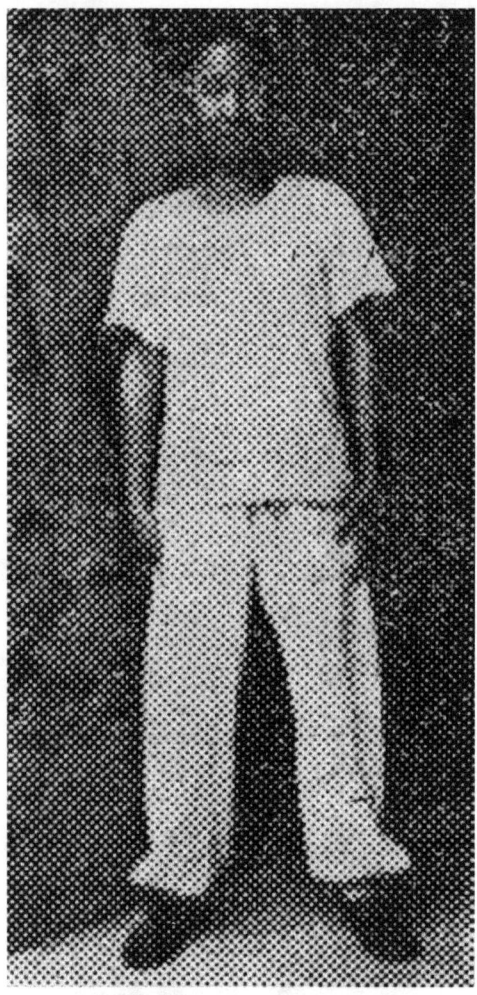

1. Head straight
2. Eyes at natural level
3. Relaxed shoulders
4. Mouth closed
5. Tongue on upper palate
6. Breath through nose
7. Collecting chi in Dan Tien
8. Feet shoulder width apart

1. *Tearing the Silk*

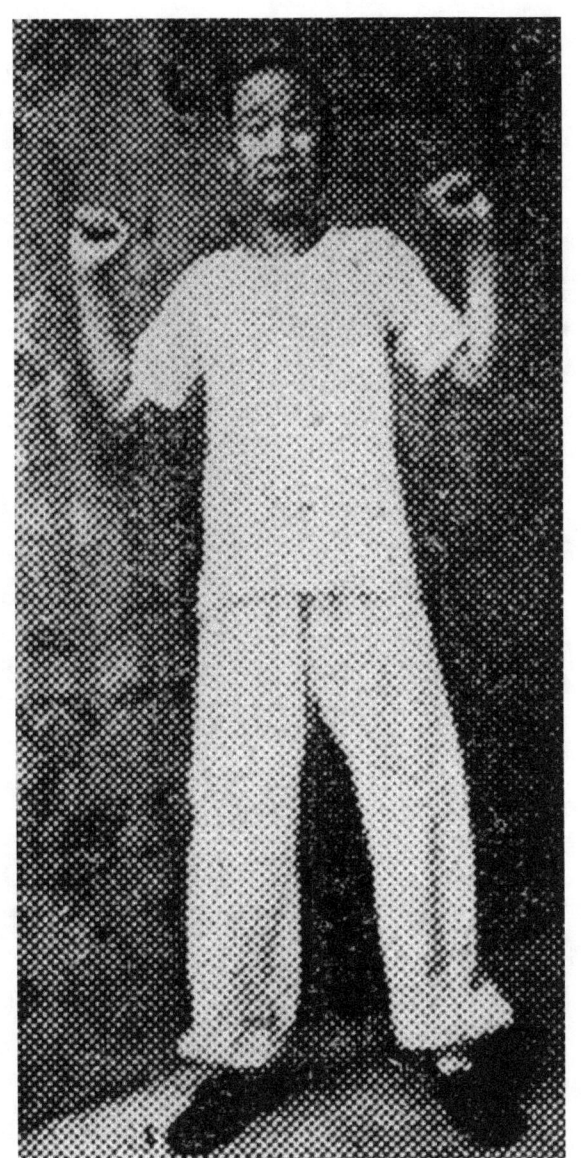

Explanation of Movement:

Opening the chest muscles, allowing the lungs to expand.

2. *Strong Lord Lifts Weight to Heaven*

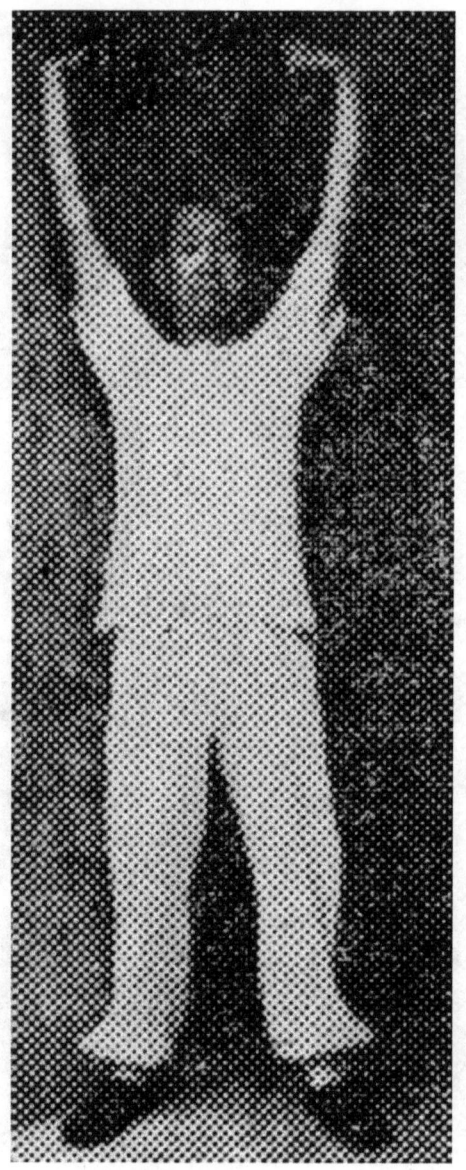

Explanation of Movement:

Improves blood and chi flow, opening many vessels or path ways of the body.

3. *Fung Hwong (Mythical Bird) Spreads Her Wings*

Explanation of Movement:

Calms the body and spirit, maintaining good health to the lungs and ribs.

4. *Immortal Reaches Towards the Heavens*

A. stretching up on tips of toes

Explanation of Movement:

Chinese philosophy of extinguishing your spiritual flame.

4. *Immortal Reaches Towards the Heavens*

B. Bending Down

Explanation of Movement:

Prevents stomach from falling into the intestines.

5. *Chief Priest of a Buddhist Temple Bends Back, Expelling the Body's Dirty Chi*

Explanation of Movement:

Expels dirty chi from stomach, exchanging it for good/healthy chi.

This also exercises the internal organs, as well as the bones of the front i.e, ribs and sternum.

6. *Open Window with Strength of Arms, Look at the Moon*

Explanation of Movement:

Exercises the shoulders, also strengthens two acupuncture points on the back called Ko-bon.

7. *Descending Posture*

(Taken from the image of a Chinese bird that descends from the sky with one wing and one leg extended.)

Explanation of Movement:

This improves the health and flexibility of the joints and tendons. It also promotes healthy blood flow and blood pressure.

8. *Riding the Horse*

Explanation of Movement:

A horseman is always in good health, even if you don't have a horse, one can be healthy by practicing, imagining riding a horse.

Chapter 11

Sitting Ba Dwan Jin (The Generation of Your own Chi)

(Common Names, Explanation of Movement and Positional Figures)

1. *Preparation*

Explanation of Movement:

Hands brace over Dan Tien, eyes closed, remain quiet/serene like still water, calm your spirit/heart (see picture), slow, deep breathing.

2. *Generating Chi by Clicking Teeth*

Explanation of Movement:

Place tongue on palate, lightly click teeth 36 times. Clicking the teeth produces saliva, swallow this saliva.

Purpose:

The teeth are bone, therefore related to the kidneys. If the bones are bad or vice versa, the kidneys too are bad. This exercise strengthens bones and tendons. Also, the teeth are the first contact for nutritional intake. If your teeth are in bad condition, your nutrition is bad and leads to a decline in health.

The tongue on the roof of the mouth produces saliva. Swallowing this saliva is like watering a grave stone. It cleanses the inside of the body and also follows the Chinese concept of dousing the souls "fire."

One's saliva prolongs the life which is a Chinese concept that originates from that of the tortoise. The tortoise is a creature known for tremendously long life. It is said this creature survives during the winter without eating and is able to sustain itself by collecting and swallowing its own saliva. For this reason saliva is known as "long life wine". A person who spits is believed to be shortening/depleting their life.

3. Washing Face, Beating Drum

Explanation of Movement:

1. First rub hands until very warm, then like washing one's face, rub your hands against your face. Thoroughly cover every crease and curve of one's face.

2. Place your hands flat against your ears and press tightly. Then release, you should feel a pressure release. Do this several times.

3. With your index and middle finger "twiddle" tap the left side of the nape of the neck (base of the skull) with left hand 34 times, then repeat same thing on right side also 34 times.

Purpose:

Humans naturally generate energy. Massaging the orifices, cavities of the face is therapeutic. In acupuncture, needles are used to stimulate points but the faces' cavities are shallow, therefore massage rather than needles are sufficient. Rubbing the skin also assists in sloughing off dead or dirty skin, allowing skin of the face to grow anew and beautify.

The ear "popping" is good for strengthening hearing.

Hitting the "drum" clears the head, stimulates the brain and increases attention, which is a result of increasing the blood flow to the brain.

4. *Embracing the Shoulders and Turning*

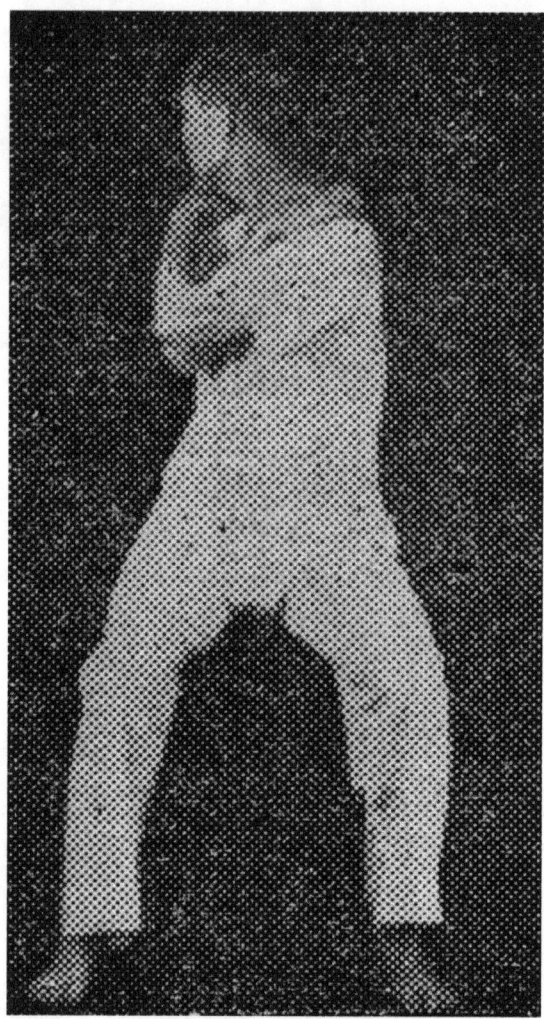

Explanation of Movement:

1. Posture: embrace one's shoulders and turning from side to side.

2. There is a pressure point along the shoulder, while turning slowly, do this 10-15 times. (This is an area that medicine or needles can't reach. So an individual must do it themselves. Not only does it heal one's body, but it exercises the chest, abdomen, waist and hips).

5. *Massaging Both Kidney Points*

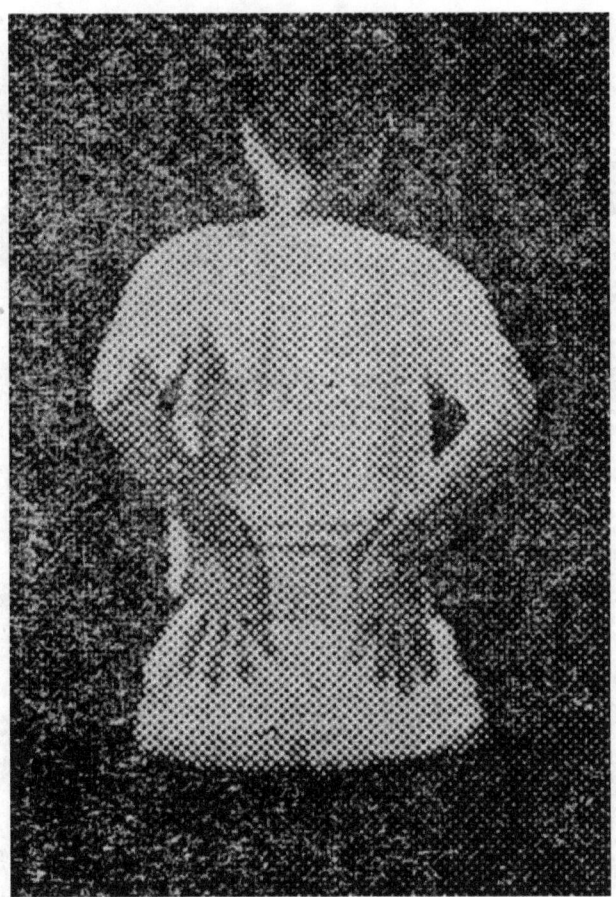

Explanation of Movement:

1. Posture: the kidney points are right above the hip bone in the back

2. First gather chi in the Dan Tien, rub hands till warm, then massage the kidney point 36 times.

3. The kidney points should become warm. Many reasons why humans have lower back pain is related to the kidney point being "cold". (The Tao or Yin/Yang Chinese healing concepts) "Cold" is taken to mean "weak", applying heat strengthens this and heals the point.

6. *Massaging Between the End of the Spine and Tailbone*

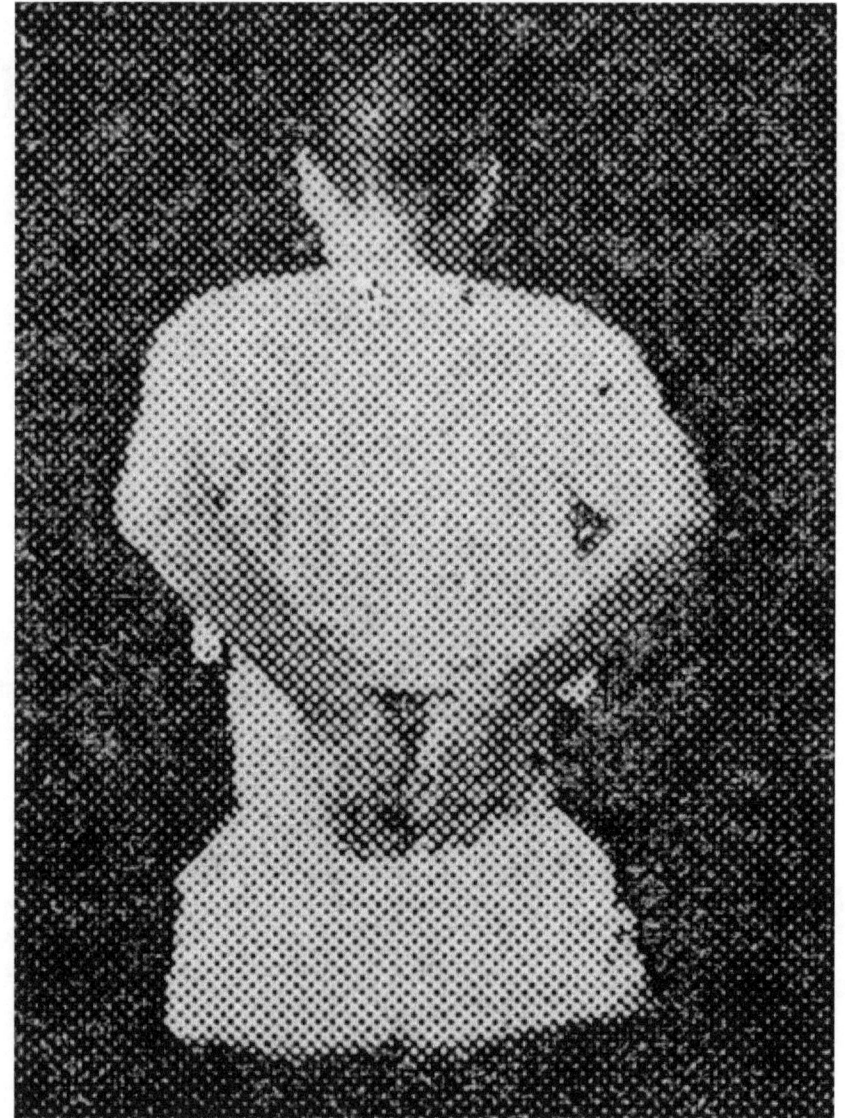

Explanation of Movement:

1. Using both middle fingers massage this area until it is warm/hot.

2. Doing this heals/helps the entire body's blood flow.

7. *Massaging the Dan Tien*

Explanation of Movement:

1. First collect chi into the Dan Tien. Tighten the pelvic floor to prevent chi from escaping the Dan Tien.

2. With both hands rub in circular motions (clockwise) until hot. Do this slowly.

3. Prevents hemorrhoids.

8. *Massaging the Yon-chen*

(Pressure point on the foot.)

Explanation of Movement:

1. Massage this pressure point on the foot 36 times until hot.

2. This point connects to both blood and chi flow throughout the body. The body's "fire" is doused. In the winter the feet can remain warm. Coordination also improves.

Closing Note

Method: Wake up and complete this entire process (Generating your own Chi). Before turning in repeat this process a second time

If this is done daily:

- it is shown persons hard of hearing regain some hearing

- lower back pain is relieved

- sinus pressure is relieved

- reduces hypertension

- reduces stress

Chapter 12

General Introduction to Sword Skill

Sword skill is the most revered martial arts skill in Chinese history, because the practice is so high and noble. Many people know how to do it, but they don't have a true understanding of it. Gradually, it has become mystical. There have been one or two who possessed such unique techniques and high levels of skill that they were viewed as gods of sword skill. However, they treasured their skills so highly that they were unwilling to share them with others. We are also short of reference books on this subject. Due to these factors, sword skill has become nearly extinct; our most precious art is unable to propagate.

In ancient times there were many emperors and nobles who were great swordsmen, of whom only their names are known. Further research is very difficult. History books show us that many famous people relied on the sword to accomplish their goals. For example, Tsao Moa robbed the noble Han Gong using sword skill, so that his country, Lu, was not attacked. Then Mau Suay, with his sword, rebuked the noble Tsu Zhi, gaining respect for his country. The emperor Gau Tzu used a three foot sword to gain his empire. The noble Tsu Di got up every morning at the crowing of the cock to practice sword in order to protect his country.

All the nobles made their swords by hand. This required much concentration. No other instrument could compare with the sword. That is why in ancient times the sword was a sign of nobility.

Sword skill follows the law of nature. The hand must follow the will of the heart. There are many dynamic forms in sword skill. The methods of sword skill may be divided up into sixteen techniques: stabbing, splitting, chopping, lifting, scooping, chopping and pulling toward you, touching, tossing, blocking, hanging up, charging, twisting, pulling back, peeling, holding, and circling. The hands, eyes and body must follow the movements of the feet: forwards, backwards, side stepping and turning. The strength comes from the mind. If you practice long enough, you will develop sword skill.

Chapter 13

Explanation of Sword Skill Techniques and Their Functions

Sword skill contains six pairs of "oneness".

The three inward items are as follows:

- Heart and mind are one
- Mind and chi are one
- Chi and strength are one

The three outward items are:

- Eye and sword are one
- Sword and footsteps are one
- Footsteps and body are one

The whole body is smooth and balanced. The living strength of sword skill is in the continuous flow of chi and in the concentration to emit it.

The function (application) of sword skill has sixteen techniques.

1. The sword tip extends straight forward. This is called stabbing (tsyh).

2. The body of the sword strikes downward to chop. This is called chopping (kan).

3. The body of the sword cuts obliquely from the left top down to the right, or from the right top down to the left. This is called splitting (pi).

4. Flick the wrist upward to make the tip and the body of the sword follow from downward to upward. This is called plucking (tiao).

5. With one hand flick the wrist in a backward motion on the side of the body to make the sword tip go up. This is called a slide block and cut (liao).

6. Back and forth sawing motion is called sawing (chou).

7. The body of the sword is flat and horizontal. This is called touching (mou).

8. The body of two swords are held out parallel. This is called tossing (pou).

9. The sword is held straight up. This is called puncturing upward (tsong).

10. The body of the sword is oblique and horizontal. This is called blocking (lan).

11. The tip of the sword hangs down. This is called hanging (gua).

12. The body of the sword blocks horizontally upward. This is called upholding (tou).

13. Swing the sword tip (like a pendulum) from left to right or right to left. This is called swinging (giau).

14. Partial cut with the sword tip. This is called peeling (shao).

15. Five fingers press the handle of the sword to make the tip of the sword bounce up. This is called retreating and lifting (pong).

16. The tip of the sword spins around. This is called sweeping or clouding [obscuring] (yun).

These are basic ideas and definitions. Every technique is further divided into several movements. Each posture is explained in detail.

Every movement is clearly distinct. Once you become familiar with them, they will "flow" smoothly. The applications of the variations exist in the heart.

I write this Tai Chi Sword book primarily for the art. Application is secondary. Anytime a learner is watchful and ready to understand, the art and its application will naturally become one.

After practicing a long time, you will enter an indescribable, wonderful realm.

Chapter 14

Introduction to Tai Chi Sword

Common sword skill is mostly made of fast moves, like a fish diving in the water, or a flying bird. It is like the blowing wind, with lightning quick moves, with fast moving eyes and steps to match the speed of the sword. Sixteen different sword techniques make up the basis for common sword skill; that which consists of a hard and strong form.

The practice of Tai Chi Sword, however, is more than that. Every move follows the form of the Tai Chi Diagram (Yin/Yang symbol) and its meaning. The sword tip follows the Tai Chi figure.

Learning Tai Chi Sword is no different from learning Tai Chi Chuan. It follows the Tai Chi movement and its quietness. It is empty (calming and meditative) and also real (having application), focusing and concentrating on the coordination of the hands and feet.

The sword follows the intention of the mind, the heart is relaxed, the hands stable. Hardness is transformed into tenderness, and application into form.

Back and forth movement is ordered, observing the changes and opportunities (of the opponent).

If the movement only has hardness without tenderness, the method is a dead form, not dynamic.

Tai Chi Sword uses quietness to control the moves, and tenderness to combat hardness.

There are four methods used in Tai Chi Chuan: sticking, supporting, adhering, and following. These methods are also very important in Tai Chi Sword.

All movements are according to the sixteen basic techniques, and follow the Tai Chi yin/yang figure. Forward and backward movements are very graceful, and have a continuous movement and flow of Chi. The changes in sword movement are not to be separated from these principles.

In writing this book, I will give every posture both a technical name to describe the meaning and the art, as well as a generic name which explains the application of the movement. I also show figures of each posture for reference.

Chapter 15

Hints for the Practice of Tai Chi Sword

- If you want to practice Tai Chi Sword, the best way is to first practice Tai Chi Chuan, because every movement contains the idea of the Tai Chi figure. If you practice Tai Chi Chuan for your basis, then it will be very easy for you to learn Tai Chi Sword. The turning, changing, form, figure and steps of Tai Chi Sword are very similar to those of Tai Chi Chuan. So if you want to practice Tai Chi Sword, it is best to first practice Tai Chi Chuan.

- No matter what you do, you must be persistent. Learning Tai Chi Sword is no exception. In the beginning it is hard, but to be persistent is even harder. You must keep the spirit of honesty and purity, empty yourself, and do your best to research and try to understand. Eventually you will become skillful.

- Sword practice requires the use of the "secret sword". If the left hand holds the real sword, the right hand fingers are held in secret sword position, and vice versa. Secret sword requires bending the thumb, ring finger, and little finger together, while the index and middle fingers are held out straight, and pressed together to show sincerity. The sword follows the finger, enhancing the power of the sword. It also shows the art and spirit of Tai Chi Sword.

- When first beginning to practice sword, use a sword made of wood or bamboo until your steps, body and hands all find a "doorway". Then you may change to a real sword. The length of the sword when held with the 'backhanded' left hand should be such that the tip of the sword is even with the top of the head.

Chapter 16

Order and Names of Each Posture of Tai Chi Sword

LIST OF POSTURES

1. Preparation
2. Fung Hwong (Bird) Spreads Wings[1]
3. Immortal Points the Way
4. Three Rings Around the Sun
5. Turn Head to Look at the Moon
6. Yin Yang Tai Chi Posture
7. Shooting the Wild Goose
8. Major Literary Star[2]
9. Turquoise Dragon Emerges from the Sea
10. Horizontal Chop Behind
11. Left and Right Sweeping Cut (#1)
12. Left and Right Sweeping Cut (#2)
13. Left and Right Sweeping Cut (#3)
14. Minor Literary Star[3]
15. Rainbow Sword Pierces the Sun
16. Dividing the Grass in Search of the Snake
17. Sword Inside the Fish's Body[4]
18. Wild Cat Catches the Mouse
19. Fung Hwong Raises Her Head
20. Yellow Bee Enters the Cave (Part 1 - circling)
21. Yellow Bee Enters the Cave (Part 2 - entering)
22. Minor Literary Star

---

[1] Fung Hwong is the mythical bird wife of the dragon emperor.
[2] Great calligrapher draws star on a vertical surface.
[3] Lesser calligrapher draws star on a horizontal surface.
[4] A legendary assassin was able to sneak a sword into the emperor's presence by hiding it in the gullet of a large fish.

23. Rainbow Sword Pierces the Sun
24. Giant Eagle Spreads Its Wings
25. Tai Kung (Old Gentleman) Fishing[5]
26. Tiger Walks to the Right and Left on the Dragon Path (#1)
27. Tiger Walks to the Right and Left on the Dragon Path (#2)
28. Tiger Walks to the Right and Left on the Dragon Path (#3)
29. Embrace the Moon
30. Birds Fly Into the Woods
31. Black Dragon Shakes out Its Tail
32. Turquoise Dragon Emerges From the Sea
33. Wind Rolls Up the Lotus Leaf
34. Lion Turns Head to the Left and Right
35. Tiger Holds Its Head
36. Wild Horse Leaps the Water Gate
37. Rein in the Horse
38. Compass Points to the South
39. Walk Left and Right Into the Wind to Sweep the Dust (#1)
40. Walk Left and Right Into the Wind to Sweep the Dust (#2)
41. Walk Left and Right Into the Wind to Sweep the Dust (#3)
42. Walk Left and Right Into the Wind to Sweep the Dust (#4)
43. Major Literary Star
44. Wheels to the Left and Right
45. Wheels Turning Backwards
46. Shooting Star Chases the Moon
47. Fung Hwong Nods Head Three Times
48. Crane Turns Body
49. Emperor Kills Giant Snake With Sword
50. Willow Branches Bend Behind
51. Swallow Enters Its Nest (Part 1)
52. Swallow Enters Its Nest (Part 2)
53. At the River's Edge, Look at the Moon
54. Point to the Sunrise in the East
55. Er Lang (Second Son) Carries the Mountain[6]
56. Incense Stick Points Up to Heaven

---

[5] Tai Kung was a famous fisherman who held his bait above the surface of the water and the fish would leap out to take it.

[6] Er Lang, nephew of the Jade Emperor (of heaven), who's strength and power enabled him to carry mountains on a pole across his shoulders, and imprison Sun Wukong, (the Monkey King) under a mountain.

57. Wind Sweeps the Plum Blossom (Part 1)
58. Wind Sweeps the Plum Blossom (Part 2)
59. Hold Up the Tablet[7]
60. Finish - Return to Beginning Posture

---

[7] When local chieftains wanted to petition the emperor, they would go to the audience hall with their standards, or tablets of office, and hold them up to attract the attention of the emperor.

Chapter 17

Foot Step and Directional Figures

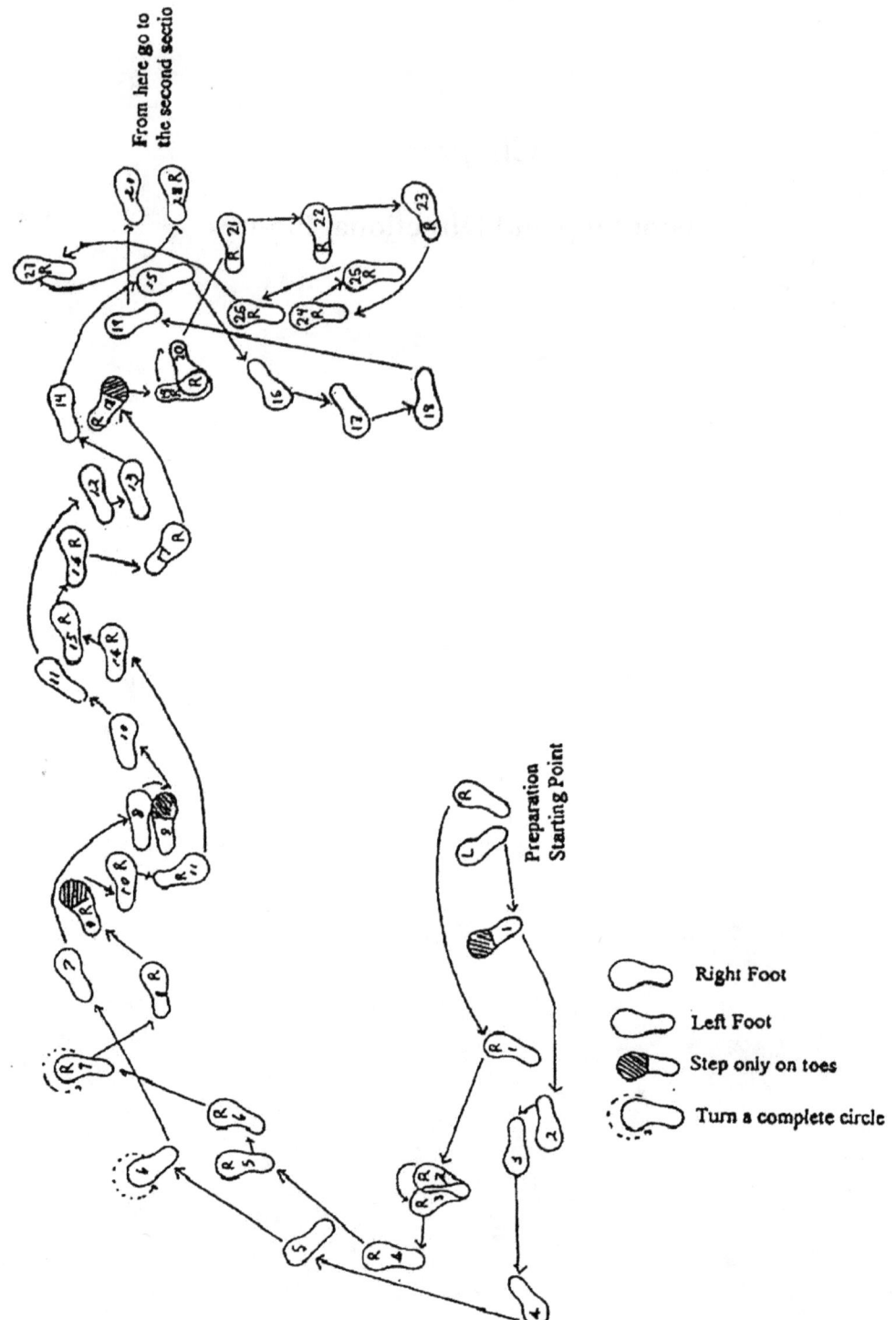

Figure 1 Explanation:

1. The first section of the path of the footsteps start from the preparation until the thirty seventh position.

2. The entire path is divided into two sections in the figure in order to avoid over lapping the footsteps. Actually, the entire path should be completed continuously, (figuratively, in one breath).

3. It is not possible to show in the figure if the feet are raised or turned. To know this, you must read the explanation and see the picture of each position in chapter 18.

4. It is not possible to show in the figure if the feet are to readjust or move repeatedly. For this, please see chapter 18.

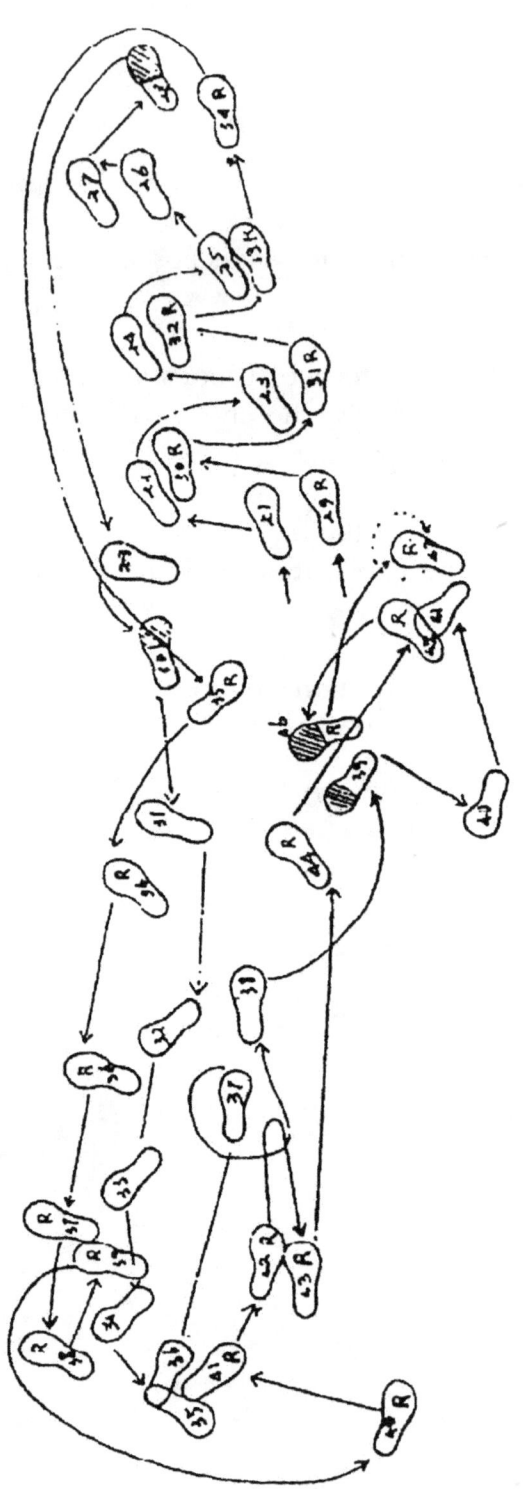

Figure 2 Explanation:

1. This second section of the form begins at position 38. Follow the pathway until finishing at position 60.

2. All the marks used in this figure are the same as the steps of the previous page.

3. When you complete all the steps of the Tai Chi Sword form, you will come back to the starting position.

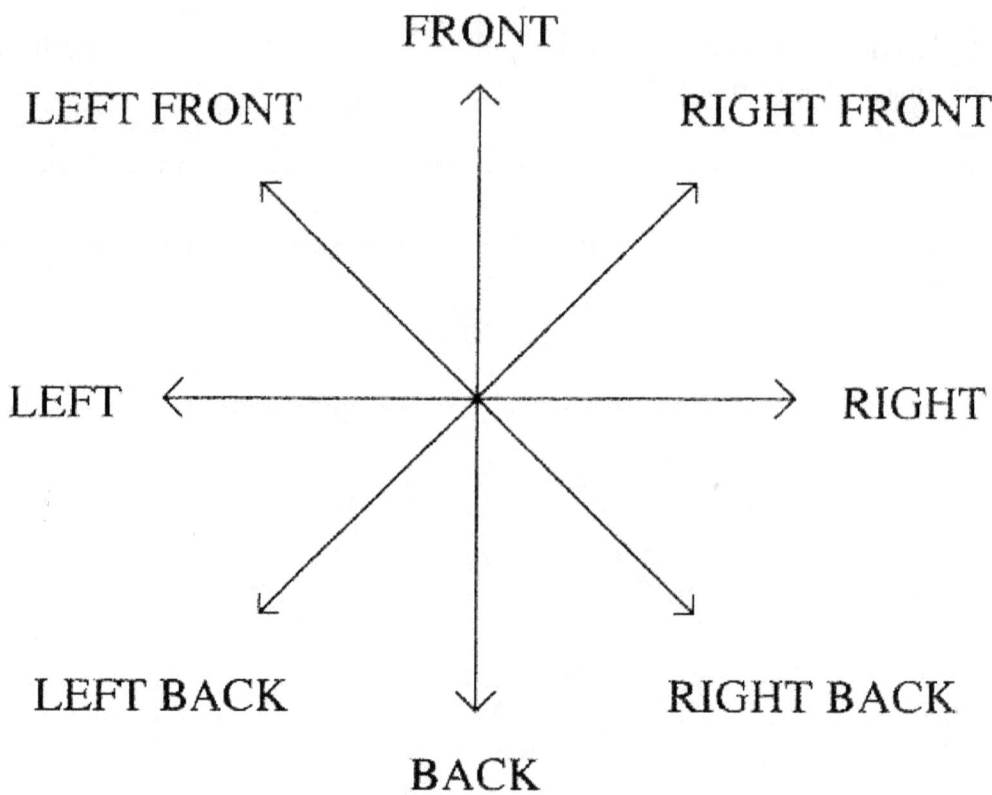

Directional Figure:

Preparation begins by facing forward. It doesn't matter how you move; your front, back, left and right are all based from the direction you presently face.

The photograph may cause you to perceive the direction differently than it actually is. Please read the explanation of the movement and observe the pathway of the footsteps.

Chapter 18

Tai Chi Sword

(Classical and Common Names of Positions,
Description of Movement and Positional Figures)*

---

* The contemporary photographs, featuring Jeffery Lee Nickel, were taken from various angles that allowed the photographer to capture all aspects of the posture. These photographs have been labeled to avoid any confusion in direction. In addition, these photographs represent the evolution of the forms over several decades, as taught by Grandmaster Yin.

1. *Preparation*

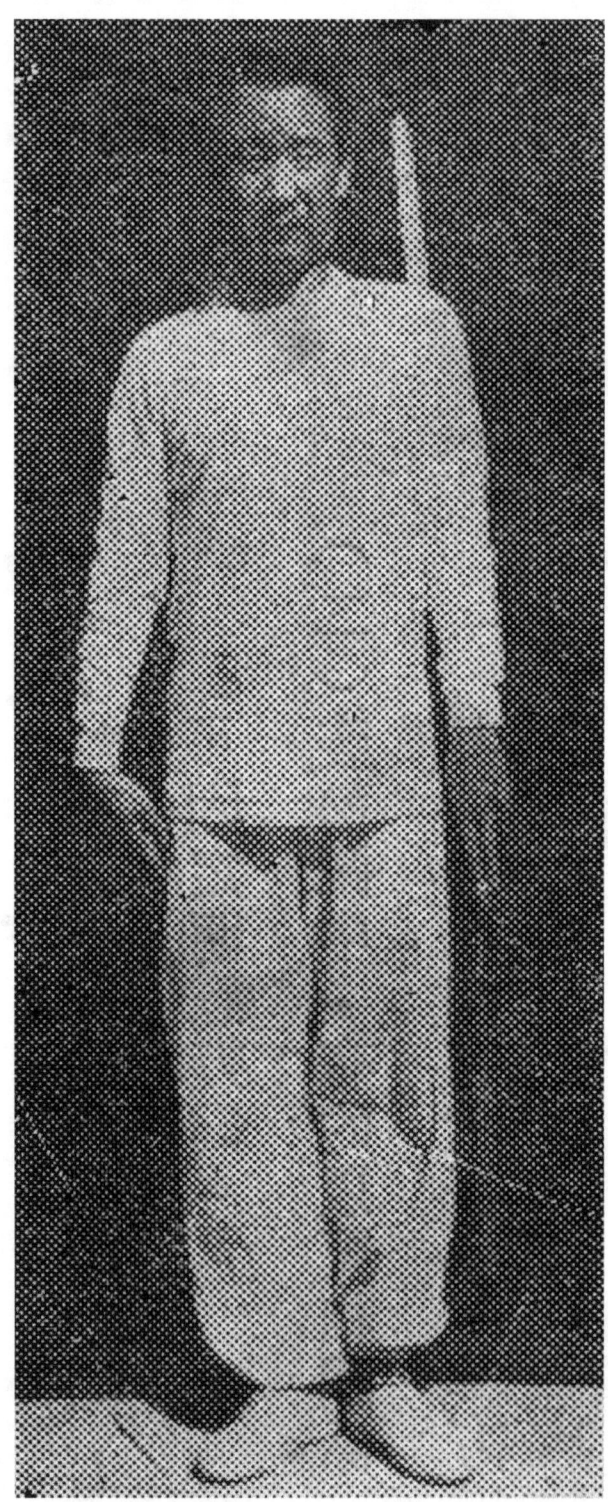

Meaning of Classical Name:

The first position before starting movement to calmly sink (chi) down.

Description of Movement:

Head and body straight, close your mouth. Sink Chi down to the Dan Tien. Eyes look straight ahead. Use your little finger, ring finger and bent thumb to hold the sword handle. Sword tip is straight up against the posterior side or your left arm. Right fingers are clasped together. Raise both hands diagonally until they meet at the top, then slowly separate them while bringing them back down.

2. *Fung Hwong (Bird) Spreads Wings*

Meaning of Classical Name:

Spread out your left and right arms slightly upwards like a bird spreading out its wings.

Common Name:

Both arms extended flat.
Move hands and feet to stand on right leg only in order to exercise strength.

Description of Movement:

Follow preparation with both arms extended flat right and left. At the same time, lift up left leg. Body weight is altogether on the right leg, facing forward.

3. *Immortal Points the Way*

Meaning of Classical Name:

Bow and arrow stance, right hand in secret sword, pointing to the upper left.

Common Name:

Brush left knee, point right hand.

Description of Movement:

Lift both arms up slightly, place left foot down and go into left bow stance at left angle. Left hand brushes knee, still holding sword against the posterior of the left arm. Right hand in secret sword points in an upper left angle. Eyes look at right hand.

4. *Three Rings Around the Sun*

Meaning of Classical Name:

The name Three Rings Around the Sun refers to the position of an upraised right leg and diagonally up and outstretched hands.

Common Name:

Kick the foot, stretch out the arms.
Kick right foot upward and stand only on left foot.

Description of Movement:

Follow the previous position by slowly raising the right foot, then kicking the foot forward. Pull back the right hand slightly, and at the same time stretch the left hand out upward and forward, so the right leg and both hands are parallel, facing the left.

5. *Turn Head to Look at the Moon*

Meaning of Classical Name:

Put the right foot back to the floor and squat down, with the right hand stretched out and holding the secret sword. Eyes follow the right finger and look up.

Common Name:

Squat down and look to the right.
Exercises and strengthens the flexibility of the legs and feet.

Description of Movement:

Place right foot back on floor and squat down, (twist sitting with left leg behind right leg.) Sweep the right hand alongside and below the body until it points up with arm stretched out to the right. The back-handed left hand holds the sword against the left arm. Slightly adjust the body so the eyes follow the angled direction of the right finger.

6. *Yin Yang Tai Chi Posture*

Meaning of Classical Name:

With the left foot, draw a large circle just above the ground. Make a large circle with the left hand. Clasp the right, (yang), and left, (yin), hands together to cause the blending of yin and yang.

Common Name:

Receiving the sword (into the right hand).
Left hand (yin) is above, right hand (yang) is below; yin and yang grasp together. The sword is transferred into the right hand to prepare for formal sword play.

Description of Movement:

Sweep the left hand out from the left back side to the upper front drawing a circle ending at the chest. At the same time, stand up from squatting position and draw another circle on the ground with the left foot, then lift it up. Bring the right hand underneath the left hand to receive the sword. Keep the right and left hands close together, while standing only on the right leg.

7. *Shooting the Wild Goose*

Meaning of Classical Name:

Right hand holds the sword; left hand holds the secret sword diagonally upward in the gesture of shooting a wild goose.

Common Name:

Puncture diagonally upward.
Right hand holds the sword. If the enemy attacks from the left side, puncture his "face door".

Description of Movement:

Left leg steps toward the left. Sink down to a low bow stance. Right hand grasps the sword, then puncture upward diagonally to the left with left hand, secret sword pointing toward the same direction. Eyes face left, looking at the tip of the sword.

8. *Major Literary Star*

Meaning of Classical Name:

Right hand holds the sword in a horizontal position, like a famous calligrapher (literary star) holding a writing brush.

Common Name:

Press down, lift up.
After puncturing the enemy's face, he returns with a low puncture. Hold down his sword, then sweep underneath his weapon and raise it above the head.

Description of Movement:

Following the previous position, the sword sweeps down, with the body following. Then back-flip the wrist to bring the sword up above the head. At the same time, the left foot lifts up, standing only on the right leg. The left hand holds secret sword just below the tip of the sword, with the eyes looking at the sword tip.

9. *Turquoise Dragon Emerges from the Sea*

Meaning of Classical Name:

The sword tip slowly comes out from the lower back part of the body until it rises above the head top. Thus the name describes the movement.

Common Name:

Following the force and then puncture.
The enemy attacks from the right side; Use the sword to chop it and press it down. Then throw the body, (full rotation of the hip) to the enemy coming from the left side. Sword punctures diagonally upward.

Description of Movement:

Following the previous position, the sword chops back and down, while the left foot steps forward into bow stance. The sword presses down, and the body is thrown (shifting weight and turning) towards the left side. The sword comes out from the lower back of the body, puncturing diagonally upwards towards the left side. The left hand holding the secret sword is above, to protect the head. The left leg is the bow, the right leg the arrow, (bow and arrow, or bow stance). The sword tip comes out above the head top. Eyes looking at the tip of the sword, to the left.

10. *Horizontal Chop Behind*

Meaning of Classical Name:

Twist the body and turn the head back. Sword sweeps in an arc from the upper left side to horizontal position on the right side.

Common Name:

Turn back and chop horizontally.
The previous motion was a thrust to the upper left. Then an enemy attacks from the right. Twist the body, rotating back to chop, placing the sword horizontal to block the enemy.

Description of Movement:

Follow the previous position with a bodily rotation, turning the head back. Chop horizontally behind. The left hand follows the right hand, at the same time, move into bow and arrow stance, right leg in front, (the bow) left leg behind, (the arrow). Face toward the right side.

11. *Left and Right Sweeping Cut (#1)*

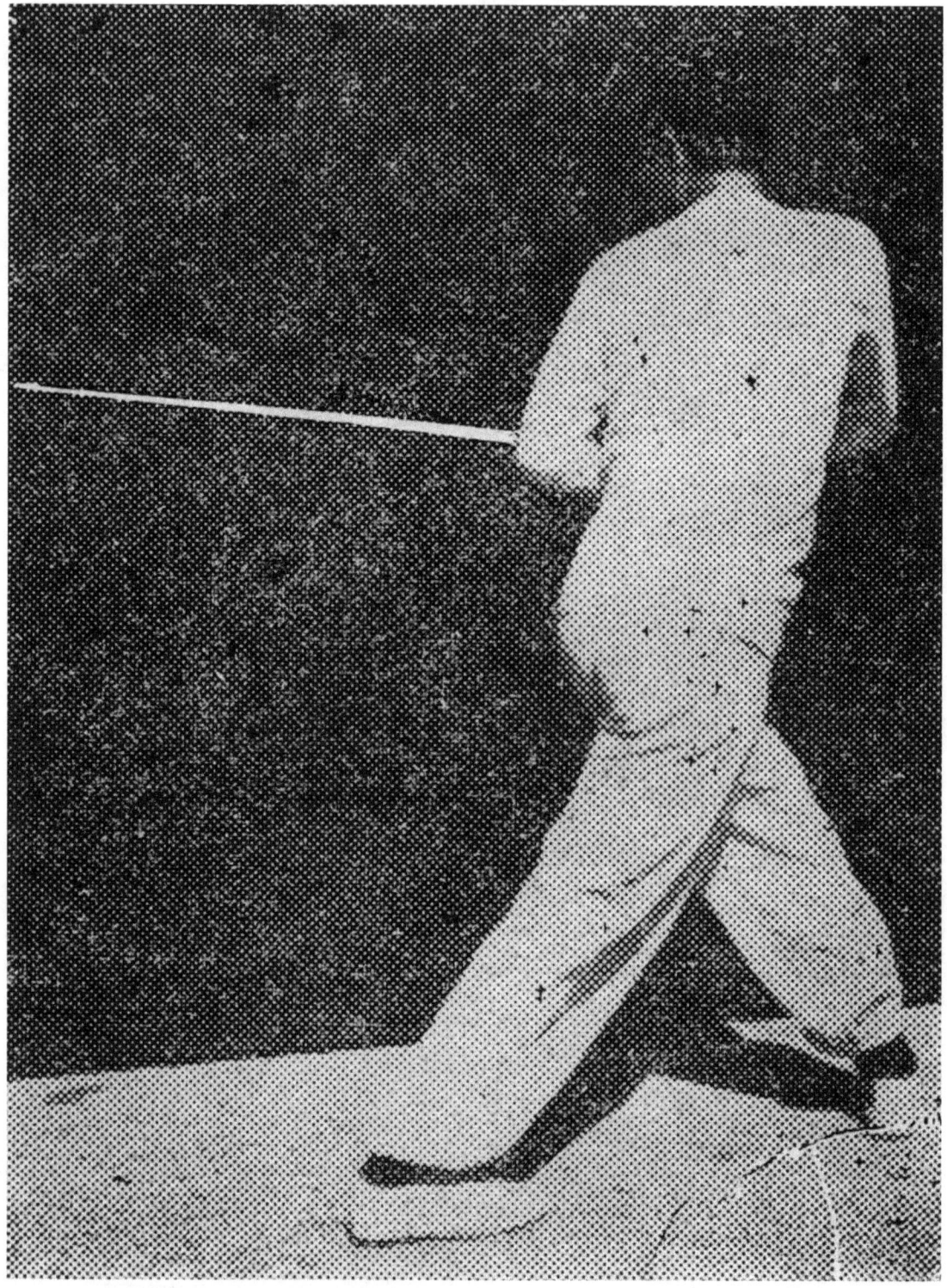

* Photographed From Different Angle

Meaning of Classical Name:

Circle around once with the sword held horizontal for cutting.

Common Name:

Same as formal name.
Turn back to block. The enemy is all around. Hold sword horizontally to protect the body while sweeping around. Palm up is yang sword; palm down is yin sword.

Description of Movement:

Left hand covers the right hand while holding the sword in a horizontal position. From the right side, turn around once to sweep-cut (palm up), coming back to face the right. Use the two feet as a pivot to turn into a crossed leg position, the sword still stretched out to the right, and the left hand still covering the right hand. The body is slightly twisted at an angle. Look over the left shoulder.

12. *Left and Right Sweeping Cut (#2)*

Meaning of Classical Name:

Beginning from the last position, turn around to sweeping cut from left to right.

Common Name:

Same as formal name.
First sweeping cut from right to left. Sweeping cut again from left to right to protect the body, leaving no room for the enemy to attack.

Description of Movement:

Turn the sword hand so the palm is facing down. Now the sword becomes a yin sword. Sweeping cut from left to right. At the same time step the right foot forward one step to the left, the sword following the body as it turns back to the right. Use both feet as a pivot, turning into a cross position, slightly crouched down. Extend the left hand toward the left, and face the right.

13. *Left and Right Sweeping Cut (#3)*

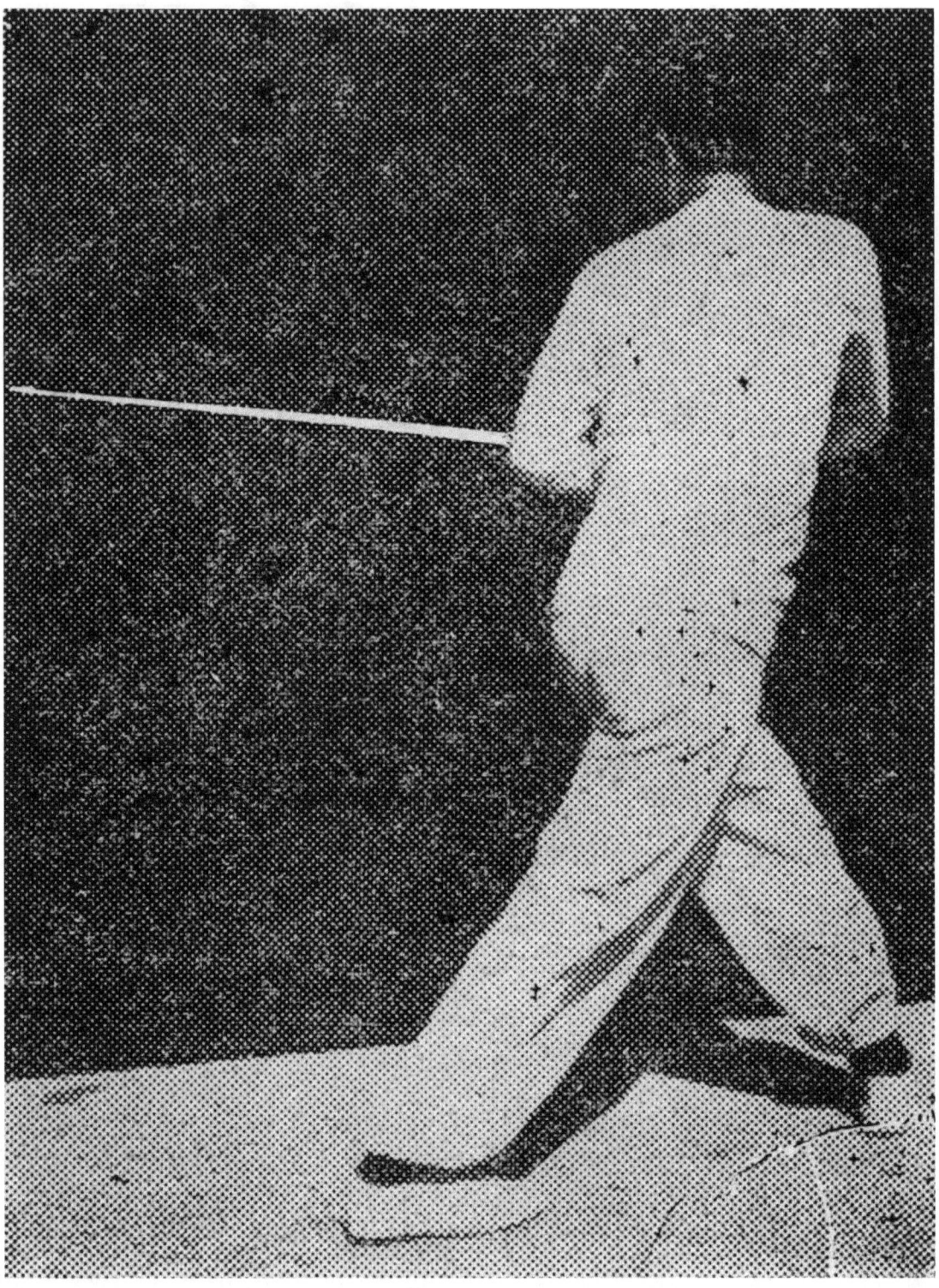

*** Photographed From Different Angle**

Description of Movement:

Turn the right palm over back to yang sword. With the left leg, step forward. Bring the left hand back to cover the right hand. The position and movement is the same as #11.

14. *Minor Literary Star*

*** Photographed From Different Angle**

Meaning of Classical Name:

This position is quite similar to the Major Literary Star, except that the tip of the sword points down. Because the position is downward, it is called minor. (The more talented calligrapher can paint on a vertical surface, with the brush held horizontal to the ground, but the less talented, or minor star, must have the writing surface held flat, with the brush vertical, to prevent dripping of the ink.)

Common Name:

Hanging upside down, pick up and block.
The enemy attacks the lower part of the body from the right side. Pick up the sword and use it to block. It hangs with the sword tip downward, protecting the body.

Description of Movement:

Bring the sword down, make a "sword flower" movement (back-flip the wrist, circle back with hilt leading), then pick it up again, letting it hang upside down. The right leg steps forward toward the left. Then raise the left leg, facing toward the left.

15. *Rainbow Sword Pierces the Sun*

* Photographed From Different Angle

Meaning of Classical Name:

The sword points straight up, towards the sun. The sword movement looks like a long rainbow.

Common Name:

Straight up puncture.
The body of the sword goes up to dislodge the enemy's weapon. The sword tip punctures straight up. Look for an opportunity to attack.

Description of Movement:

Turn the right wrist upward, with the sword following upward until it becomes a straight line. The right leg is still standing independently. Point up with the left hand parallel to the right arm. Face the left front corner.

16. *Dividing the Grass in Search of the Snake*

Meaning of Classical Name:

The sword moves diagonally from a high to a low position, then goes horizontally flat toward the outside of the right leg. The movement looks like you are chopping long grass.

Common Name:

Outstretched leg, (descending posture) followed by a sweeping cut.
The sword, coming from the straight up position follows the momentum of the outstretched leg, so that the force is full and fierce. Sweep cut the enemy's foot.

Description of Movement:

Follow the previous position with the left leg coming down in front of the right leg, then the right leg steps out from behind the left leg and stretches forward. The sword follows the right leg, sweep-cutting past the right foot. The left hand points up diagonally toward the left to reinforce (counter-balance) the chop.

17. *Sword Inside the Fish's Body*

* Photographed From Different Angle

Meaning of Classical Name:

This position follows the rising of the right leg. The sword is hidden beside the inside of the right leg; only the tip of the sword is exposed beyond the foot. This name is given because the leg is used to hide the body of the sword.

Common Name:

Raised leg with hidden sword.
Raise the right leg and bring the sword back to hide it beside the right leg. This disturbs the enemy's vision as you prepare to attack.

Description of Movement:

The sword rises up with the right leg straight out and flat. The body of the sword is hidden along the right leg, only the tip of the sword is beyond the foot. The left hand holds the sword together with the right hand. Stand on left leg alone, facing the left front.

18. *Wild Cat Catches the Mouse*

* Photographed From Different Angle

Meaning of Classical Name:

Leap forward with the leg. The sword tip is thrust upward, then punctures downward, like a cat pouncing on a mouse; the body jumps up before coming down to catch the mouse.

Common Name:

Thrust upward and puncture downward.
To attack the enemy's lower part, first fake toward the upper part and then actually puncture the lower part. Because the sword is coming down, it has more force.

Description of Movement:

The right foot comes down from a jump. The left foot follows, leaping forward. The sword fakes an upward thrust, the right foot steps forward and the sword comes down from above to puncture. The right leg steps forward into bow stance, (left leg is the arrow). The left hand protects the head. The body faces forward.

19. *Fung Hwong Raises Her Head*

Meaning of Classical Name:

Use the tip of the sword to pluck upward diagonally toward your head, which is bent forward. The left hand holds the secret sword with the fingers straight up.

Common Name:

Follow the force, then pluck upward.
The enemy breaks a downward thrust and punctures toward the shoulder. Pluck up the tip of the sword to block the enemy's weapon.

Description of Movement:

The body of the sword is straight up, the sword tip is slightly angled. Bring the right leg back to a Gong Pu Bu stance, similar to a cat stance. Bring the left hand down in front of the right shoulder with the fingers pointing up, just in front of the sword. Face toward the left front corner.

20. *Yellow Bee Enters the Cave (Part 1 - Circling)*

Meaning of Classical Name:

The tip of the sword follows the turning of the body, like a bee entering a cave.

Common Name:

Protect the body, turn and puncture.
The body of the sword turns to, and protects, the chest. The sword tip is pointed forward and downward diagonally in preparation for puncturing.

Description of Movement:

The sword protects the chest, and follows the turning of the body. Both standing legs are crossed. Turn the body to face forward and pull the sword handle up diagonally. The sword tip is in front of the chest, and the left hand points forward in front of the sword tip. The eyes look at the sword tip. (Walk in a counter-clockwise circle, eight steps.)

21. *Yellow Bee Enters the Cave (Part 2 - Entering)*

* Photographed From Different Angle

Meaning of Classical Name:

Both hands hold the sword handle straight forward, standing only on the left leg. The right leg kicks behind, slightly upward. The movement is like a yellow bee entering a cave.

Common Name:

Turn and puncture low.
Two hands hold the sword together; puncture toward the enemy's lower part (gate); right leg is raised up in back to enhance the force (counter-balance).

Description of Movement:

Follow the previous position by turning (with an adjusting step) the body again, use the left leg as a hinge, turning straight forward. Two hands holding the sword, puncture straight forward, (to lower gate), the right leg raised up in back to enhance the force. Left leg supports the weight of the body. Face forward with the head slightly raised up.

22. *Minor Literary Star*

* Photographed From Different Angle

Description of Movement:

The right foot comes back down. Point the sword back in a backhanded position. Please refer to position #14, only this time face the right instead of the left.

23. *Rainbow Sword Pierces the Sun*

Description of Movement:

Turn the right wrist upward, with the sword following upward until it becomes a straight line. The right leg is still standing independently. Point up with the left hand parallel to the right arm. Face the right back corner.
Please refer to position #15, only this time face right instead of left.

24. *Giant Eagle Spreads Its Wings*

Meaning of Classical Name:

Chop (pi), toward the right, with the left hand stretched up, (to the left), as if opening the wings.

Common Name:

Follow the force, then chop diagonally.
If the enemy attacks, seize the opportunity to chop downward diagonally, with the left hand stretched upward toward the left to help the force.

Description of Movement:

With the left foot, step out to the left into a bow stance. Stretch the left hand upward toward the left. At the same time, chop down diagonally toward the right. The right foot is the arrow. Eyes look at the tip of the sword.

25. *Tai Kung (Old Gentleman) Fishing*

Meaning of Classical Name:

Bend forward at the waist while squatting down in the legs. Hold the sword as if fishing with a fishing pole.

Common Name:

Slide block and cut.
From the former position, (i.e. Giant Eagle Spreads Wings), move to counter an enemy's attack to the abdomen; pull hands and sword in to block. Chop the sword upward, using the sword tip to slide block and cut the enemy's wrist.

Description of Movement:

Pull back the sword toward the abdomen to block. Then turn the wrist backhanded, causing the sword tip to slide block and cut. At the same time, bring back the right leg close to the left leg, flexing the right leg slightly. Bring the left hand back to attach to the handle of the sword. Eyes look at the sword tip, facing toward the right.

26. *Tiger Walks to the Right and Left on the Dragon Path (#1)*

* Photographed From Different Angle

Meaning of Classical Name:

Squat and walk diagonally to the right, with the sword following your steps. Steps move in the shape of a triangle.

Common Name:

Move right to destroy the enemy.
Tilt the sword toward the enemy, moving diagonally toward the right.

Description of Movement:

Make one half sword flower counter-clockwise on the right of the body. Then, holding the sword with the tip pointed upward, and left hand (secret sword) attached to the right wrist, advance three steps to the right diagonal. Squat down on the two legs with the sword held diagonally upward.

27. Tiger Walks to the Right and Left on the Dragon Path (#2)

Meaning of Classical Name:

Squat down and step diagonally toward the left.

Common Name:

Step left to destroy the enemy.
The front edge (finger blade) of the sword is still leading. The body follows the steps diagonally toward the left to destroy and block the enemy.

Description of Movement:

Make one half sword flower clockwise on the left of the body while emptying the left foot. Then, holding the sword diagonally across the body, tip pointed upward, advance three steps to the left diagonal. Squat down feet together, pushing out finger edge blade of sword.

28. *Tiger Walks to the Right and Left on the Dragon Path (#3)*

* Photographed From Different Angle

Meaning of Classical Name:

Make one half of a sword flower. The body moves toward the right diagonally, the same as position #26.

29. *Embrace the Moon*

*** Photographed From Different Angle**

Meaning of Classical Name:

Make one sword flower clock-wise on the left and pull back the sword diagonally toward the knee, as if embracing the moon.

Common Name:

Protect the body while waiting for an opportunity to strike.
The sword tip is up, hiding in front of the chest, waiting for the opportunity to puncture the enemy.

Description of Movement:

Step back with the left leg 1/2 step. Slightly pull back the right leg, emptying the foot, ready to activate. At the same time, make a sword flower (clock-wise on the left side of body) and pull the sword back toward the right knee. The sword tip points diagonally upward.

30. *Birds Fly Into the Woods*

Meaning of Classical Name:

The sword tip points straight forward, downward and flat. Slowly bring the sword up over head height, like a bird, flying into the woods.

Common Name:

Puncture downward and pluck upward.
Step out with the right leg into a bow stance. Puncture forward, low, then pluck it upward to block the enemy's weapon which is attacking the upper body.

Description of Movement:

Step forward with the right leg into bow stance. Then, body leans forward, sword punctures forward, low, and left leg raises up behind. Then, let the sword follow the body upward slowly, until upright. Stand on right leg only. Sword and secret sword both point up overhead.

31. *Black Dragon Shakes out Its Tail*

* Photographed From Different Angle

Meaning of Classical Name:

Counter clock-wise sword flower on right side. Chop (pi) downward. Left hand is overhead, the body projecting outward diagonally.

Common Name:

Following the momentum of the body, chop downward.
The enemy comes from the right. Step left and sink down. Partially extend the right leg forward while squatting on the left leg. Follow the momentum of the body and chop downward.

Description of Movement:

Make counter clock-wise sword flower on the right while stepping the left foot out. While sinking into a Gong Pu Bu stance, chop downward with sword. Body leans forward slightly, eyes look at sword tip, left hand points up overhead to help momentum.

32. *Turquoise Dragon Emerges From the Sea*

Description of Movement:

The sword circles around, while the left foot steps into bow stance. See position #9.

33. Wind Rolls Up the Lotus Leaf

Meaning of Classical Name:

With the sword held horizontally flat, touch the left arm. Make a circle with the left arm and attach it to the right wrist. The figure is like a lotus leaf blown by the wind and curled halfway.

Common Name:

Sword horizontal, touch and attack.
If the enemy is behind the back, bring the sword down to flat and horizontal, turn the body, with the the sword following against the enemy.

Description of Movement:

Make a counter clock-wise sword flower over the head and pull the sword out of the bottom of that circle into a flat, horizontal position at chest height. The sword lies flat upon the left arm, right arm is extended across the chest so that spirit sword touches right wrist. While this movement happens, raise the right leg and step toward the right into bow stance.

34. *Lion Turns Head to the Left and Right*

Meaning of Classical Name:

The sword tip cocks to the left and right, like a lion looking to one side and then the other.

Common Name:

Left and right throw-twist.
If the enemy attacks and the force cannot be immediately overcome, then use the sword to throw and twist while backing away, waiting for the opportunity to attack.

Description of Movement:

Move the left leg back one step. Then, while shifting into left bow stance, throw the right yang (palm up) sword flat toward the left. Move the right leg back one step. Then, while shifting into right bow stance, throw the left yin (palm down) sword toward the right. Repeat left step and throw. Then step right leg back one more step, keep weight in left bow stance, stretch both arms out to the sides, with palms down, (sword is yin on the right), face forward.

35. *Tiger Holds Its Head*

Meaning of Classical Name:

Embrace the sword handle with both hands. Pull back the sword in front of the chest.

Common Name:

Flat throw and pull.
If the enemy is in front, throw the sword in front of body, stepping forward with the right foot. Then pull the sword back to the chest.

Description of Movement:

Throw the sword in front of body, clock-wise in a horizontal position (body leans backwards), stepping forward with the right foot at the end of the throw. As the left and right hands embrace together, pull the sword back to the chest, shifting the weight back into left empty step, (right foot draws back slightly). Squat down in the left leg, tip of sword pointing forward, tipped up. Face forward.

36. *Wild Horse Leaps the Water Gate*

* Photographed From Different Angle

Meaning of Classical Name:

Kick and stomp the right leg forward and jump up.

Common Name:

Jump forward, chase, puncture.
If the enemy wants to flee, jump and chase after him and puncture, to stop his retreat.

Description of Movement:

Kick up under the sword blade with the right toe, then stomp the right foot down, leaping up and forward, landing on the left foot and then stepping the right foot forward again into bow stance. As the weight moves forward into bow stance, the two hands, (still holding the sword together in a flat orientation,) stretch out forward, sending the sword tip puncturing forward. Eyes look at the tip of the sword, face forward.

37. *Rein in the Horse*

Meaning of Classical Name:

Turn your body to the left, sweeping the arms around and pull the sword in toward the chest, as if drawing in the horses reins.

Common Name:

Throw sweep, rein in the sword.
If the enemy attacks from the left side, throw-sweep the sword in a large circle, turn, and pull back the sword to the chest.

Description of Movement:

Both hands hold the sword, following the body in a left turn. Pivot on the left foot, with the right leg following to turn in a large circle until facing the right side. Rein in the sword, pulling it back in front of the chest. The sword is held out flat and toward the right. At the same time, the right leg catches up to the left leg to stand upright. Face toward the right, eyes look at the tip of the sword.

38. *Compass Points to the South*

Meaning of Classical Name:

Both hands hold the sword, stretched out flat toward the right side. The blade is perfectly flat, like a compass needle, not tilting high or low.

Common Name:

Forward flat puncture.
If the enemy is in front, step forward one step and stretch out the arms with a flat sword, puncturing his chest.

Description of Movement:

The left leg takes one step forward, with the right leg following. Both arms stretch out straight; the sword is stretched out flat and straight in front of the chest. Face to the right.

39. Walk Left and Right Into the Wind to Sweep the Dust (#1)

* Photographed From Different Angle

Meaning of Classical Name:

The movement of the sword follows that of the steps, and the sword moves like the tail of an animal sweeping the dust.

Common Name:

Left and right point chop.
The tip of the sword moves toward the left following the movement of the steps, doing point chops. All movements are those of attack and break.

Description of Movement:

Following the previous position, make a half circle on the left side of the body (point chop), step forward with the left leg, right leg follow step, knees bend as you step in, sword held diagonally toward the right and forward (protects across front of body, tip at upper right, hilt at lower left).

40. *Walk Left and Right Into the Wind to Sweep the Dust (#2)*

Meaning of Classical Name:

The same as the previous position, but direction is to the right.

Common Name:

Left and right point chop.
The same as the previous position, but direction is to the right.

Description of Movement:

Starting with tip of the sword raised up to the right, make a half circle on the right side of the body (point chop), step forward with the right leg, left leg follow step, knees bend as you step in, sword held diagonally toward the left and forward, (protects across front of body, tip at upper left, hilt at lower right).

41. *Walk Left and Right Into the Wind to Sweep the Dust (#3)*

* Photographed From Different Angle

Meaning of Classical Name:

Same as previous two position, to the left.

Common Name:

Same as previous, to the left.

Description of Movement:

Following the previous position, make a half circle on the left side of the body (point chop), step forward with the left leg, right leg follow step, knees bend as you step in, sword held diagonally toward the right and forward (protects across front of body, tip at upper right, hilt at lower left).

42. *Walk Left and Right Into the Wind to Sweep the Dust (#4)*

Meaning of Classical Name:

The same as the previous position, but direction is to the right.

Common Name:

Left and right point chop.
The same as the previous position, but direction is to the right.

Description of Movement:

Starting with tip of the sword raised up to the right, make a half circle on the right side of the body (point chop), step forward with the right leg, left leg follow step, knees bend as you step in, sword held diagonally toward the left and forward, (protects across front of body, tip at upper left, hilt at lower right).

43. *Major Literary Star*

Description of Movement:

Same as position #8, but the direction is changed. The previous position faced forward, but here face the right.

44. *Wheels to the Left and Right*

Meaning of Classical Name:

Use the tip of the sword to make a circle on the left and right sides of the body.

Common Name:

Left and right, sword protecting the body.
Use the sword to make a circle on the left and right sides of the body, like large wheels, to protect the body, so that the enemy has no place to attack.

Description of Movement:

Follow the previous position by putting the left leg down. The tip of the sword follows the body with the point down, then comes up behind and over the top to make a circle protecting the body. The right leg steps forward toward the right, with the sword following the body. The tip of the sword then hangs down on the right side of the body, and is brought up and around on the right side. Repeat a wheel on each side, then bring the sword into the position of rainbow sword pierces the sun (position #15 and #23).

45. Wheels Turning Backwards

Meaning of Classical Name:

Step backwards, the tip of the sword making a circle on the left and right sides of the body.

Common Name:

Stepping backwards, sword protecting the body.
Step backwards with the left leg, the sword tip making a circle (wheel) on the left, and then the right sides to protect the whole body.

Description of Movement:

Follow the previous position, (Rainbow Sword Pierces the Sun), by stepping backwards with the left leg. The sword tip is turned downward, then comes up behind and over the top making a circle. Step backwards with the right leg, then bring the sword tip up from the lower right and over the top, making a second circle. The circle is completed with the sword tip hanging down in front of the body and the left hand in front of the chest. The left foot is empty, face to the right.

46. *Shooting Star Chases the Moon*

Meaning of Classical Name:

Chop backwards with the sword, then chop backwards again in a continuous motion. Retreat with each sword chop. Each backward chop is done as a circular sword flower.

Common Name:

Continuous circular sword chop.
When the enemy attacks, step back with the left leg. Then back chop down. If the first chop is not successful, right step across the left leg and chop with the sword again, so the enemy may not close in.

Description of Movement:

Step back with the left leg into descending posture. The sword follows, circling clockwise in front of the body and chopping downward toward the right. Left secret sword points out to the left. Step back again (retreat), with the right leg crossing over the left. Circle the sword around again, making a sword flower with the secret sword. Straighten the left hand out toward the left.

47. Fung Hwong Nods Head Three Times

* Photographed From Different Angle

Meaning of Classical Name:

The sword tip follows the foot taps every time you pause. Repeat this three times. That is why this name is given.

Common Name:

Back step to avoid the enemy.
If the enemy is pursuing, step back one step, then chop backwards to avoid him. With each chop, pause to block the enemy's weapon.

Description of Movement:

Stand up and bring the left leg out from behind the right and step to the left. Move the right leg in front and across the left leg, pointing the toe. Raise the sword to the chest, sweep it down to the right, chop three times. Pause, then step, point and chop three times a second and third time.

48. *Crane Turns Body*

Meaning of Classical Name:

Follow the previous position by twisting your body from the waist, the sword following to chop downward.

Common Name:

Victory out of failure.
The previous position failed. The enemy's pursuit was non-stop. Turn back and chop down diagonally to surprise the enemy.

Description of Movement:

The previous position was one of backing up. Twist the waist, turning the body with the sword following upward. The right leg is slightly raised, the left leg a pivot. Turn around to the right side, sword chopping down diagonally from above. The left hand is held up, protecting the head. The left leg goes into a bow stance, the right leg is the arrow behind. Face the right.

49. *Emperor Kills Giant Snake With Sword*

Meaning of Classical Name:

This image is from the story "Emperor Chops the Snake." The left hand is held in secret sword position, the right hand holds the sword by the right flank. The right leg stands alone.

Common Name:

High sword waiting for the enemy.
Hide the sword by the right flank, crane stance on the right leg, waiting to see the enemy's intention.

Description of Movement:

Draw the sword hilt in to the body, turning the hand palm up. The left hand is also brought back to protect the sword. At the same time, the right leg is brought up next to the left leg, but no weight is put on it. Then step forward (towards the right) with the right leg making a counter-clockwise circular block on the right side of the body with the sword. Raise the left leg and draw the sword back until it is half hidden under the right flank. The left hand secret sword points forward. Look at the enemy's face.

50. *Willow Branches Bend Behind*

TAI CHI SWORD

* Photographed From Different Angle

Meaning of Classical Name:

The sword tip is hanging down behind the body. The left hand follows the position of the right hand, like the branches of a willow tree hanging down.

Common Name:

Pick up and puncture backwards.
Watching the enemy in front, puncture his lower part. An attack from behind comes too suddenly to be able to turn and face it, so the tip of the sword is used to puncture backwards behind the body.

Description of Movement:

Step forward into left bow stance. The sword punctures forward at a downward angle, then is picked up to puncture behind the body. At the same time, raise up the right leg straight out in front to strengthen the force. The left hand secret sword follows the right hand and sword to point behind the body. Turn the head enough to see the tip of the sword.

51. *Swallow Enters Its Nest (Part 1)*

Meaning of Classical Name:

Twist the body and move the arms in a circular motion like a swallow entering its nest.

Common Name:

Turn the body around, holding the sword.
Raise the sword up in the air and chop down upon the enemy. Again, throw the sword down, the body following in a downward twist. End with the sword held up overhead.

Description of Movement:

Step behind with the right leg. Then, with the hilt leading, the sword circles counter-clockwise, chopping forward, down, around behind, and ending with an overhead block. As this occurs, the body is twisting and sinking down. The knees bend with the left knee tucked behind the right. The left arm is slightly bent, the secret sword pointing upward. Face forward.

52. *Swallow Enters Its Nest (Part 2)*

Meaning of Classical Name:

Follow the previous position by twisting the body again in a circular motion, like a swallow entering its nest with its tail fluttering.

Common Name:

Turn the body, chop and pick up.
The enemy approaches from the right. The sword chops down. As the body turns, backhand the sword to pluck away the enemy's weapon.

Description of Movement:

Step behind with left leg into right bow stance, facing the right, chopping downward to the right at the same time. Then shift weight back into left foot and step back with the right leg. Shift the weight to the right leg, using it as a pivot while drawing the sword back (back handing) behind the head on the right side of the body. Left hand secret sword points to sword tip. Stance is right leg empty step. Eyes look at sword tip.

53. *At the River's Edge, Look at the Moon*

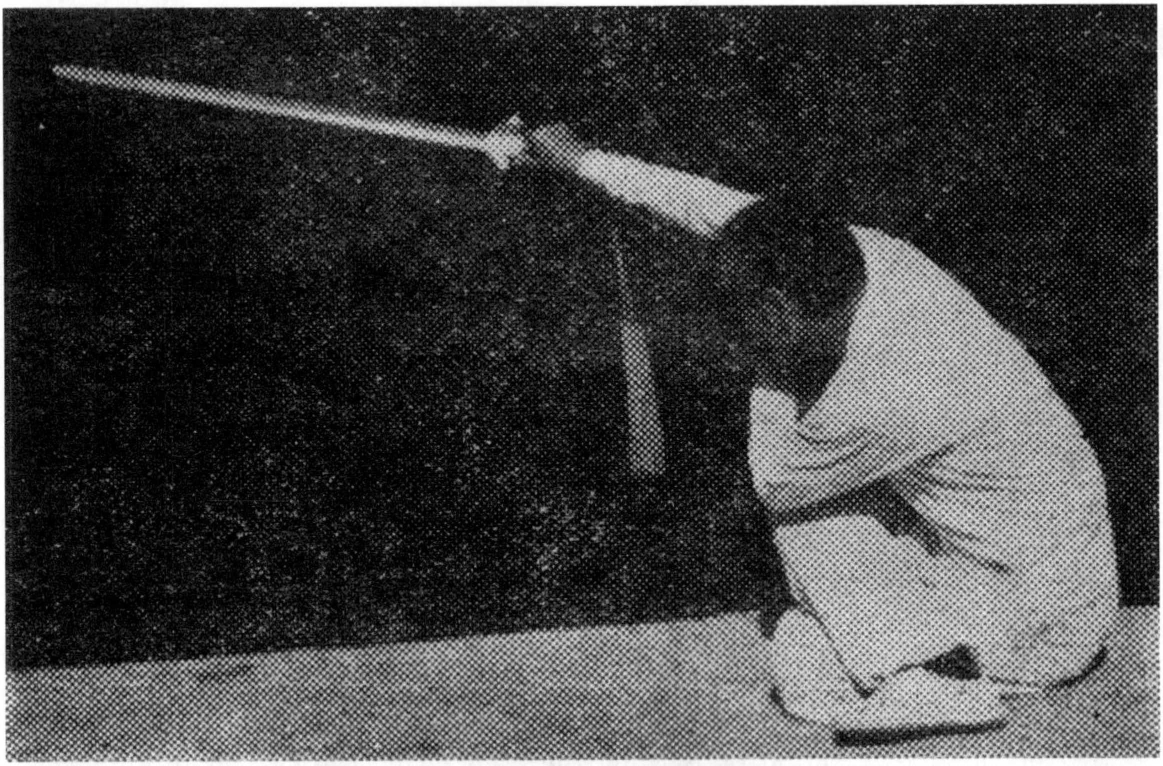

* Photographed From Different Angle

Meaning of Classical Name:

Sit down on the floor with the legs crossed. With the right hand, raise up the sword backhanded toward the upper right diagonal, (this may also be done vertical). Tilt the head to look along the sword to its tip.

Common Name:

Sit down cross legged and raise sword to puncture.
Cross the legs, twist the body to pluck up the enemy's weapon. Backhand, step forward and sit down. Raise the sword tip to puncture from below.

Description of Movement:

Adjust left foot to face the front, step right foot parallel to the left in a standing horse riding stance facing the front. As you are turning into this position, puncture straight out to the right with sword and straight out to left with left hand secret sword. Then bring the left leg behind the right and sit down cross legged. As you are sinking down, circle the sword counter-clockwise, first overhead, hilt leading, then around, down, and backhand up, twisting the body and head to look along the sword. Left hand rests on right shoulder, secret sword pointing along the sword length.

54. *Point to the Sunrise in the East*

Meaning of Classical Name:

The sword is pointed at the sunrise. Eyes gaze at the sword tip as if searching the Eastern horizon for the sunrise.

Common Name:

Pull in and hold the sword up in readiness.
Raise up the body and puncture toward the right. If the enemy plucks the sword and attacks again, pull in and uphold the sword in front of the chest to await an opportunity.

Description of Movement:

Stand up, shifting weight to left leg, then step and turn to the right into right bow stance, puncturing sword out to the right. Left hand secret sword stretches out behind, to the left. Then bring back the right leg close to the left heel. Bend both knees, holding the sword out horizontally in front of the chest, pointing to the right. The left hand secret sword touches and points along the handle. Eyes look at sword tip.

55. *Er Lang (Second Son) Carries the Mountain*

Meaning of Classical Name:

Stretch out the right and left hands, with the sword in the right hand, like a person carrying a load suspended from the ends of a pole across his shoulders.

Common Name:

Separate the hands and puncture straight out.
Separate and stretch out both hands, sword puncturing toward the right. Crane stance on the right leg.

Description of Movement:

Separate and stretch out both hands, sword puncturing toward the right, left hand secret sword puncturing to the left. Pick up left leg, crane stance on the right leg. Face forward.

56. *Incense Stick Points Up to Heaven*

Meaning of Classical Name:

The sword is toward the left, both hands holding the sword handle. The sword is held upright over the left knee. (The incense stick is held vertical and the smoke rises directly to heaven.)

Common Name:

Upright sword.
Chop the the left, then bring the sword tip back up to vertical. Look toward the left.

Description of Movement:

Step toward the left with the left leg into left bow stance. Chop the sword down from the right to the left. Raise the sword body upright over the left knee, with both hands holding the handle. Face left, eyes look at sword tip.

57. Wind Sweeps the Plum Blossom (Part 1)

Meaning of Classical Name:

Sweep the sword in a flat position.

Common Name:

Throw the sword and prepare to sweep.
Flatten the sword and draw or scrape it to the right. As the enemy approaches, use the flat sword to scrape him.

Description of Movement:

Step into right bow stance toward the right. Throw the sword flat as the body is turning to the right. Left hand secret sword also points to right. Face the right front.

58. *Wind Sweeps the Plum Blossom (Part 2)*

Meaning of Classical Name:

Raise up the left leg in back, level with the body. The right leg is a pivoting point. Starting from the right, turn in a circle with the sword sweeping all the way around.

Common Name:

Flat body sword sweep.

Description of Movement:

Continue the horizontal sweeping cut from the previous movement, raising up the left leg behind the body and pivoting on the right foot. Sword is held flat, with the arms stretched out from the body. Head is slightly raised, eyes looking at sword tip. Turn all the way around, clockwise, until facing the front again. (Try to make the pivot in five even stages, like the petals of a plum blossom.)

59. *Hold Up the Tablet*

Meaning of Classical Name:

Two hands hold the sword, with the tip pointing up. The figure looks like holding up a tablet of office, in an attitude of supplication.

Common Name:

Stand straight and still.
Sword play is now finished. Both hands hold the sword. Focus on the sword body.

Description of Movement:

Bring the left leg down against the right leg. Knees are straight. Bring the sword in front of the chest. The left hand joins the right hand in holding the sword handle. The body leans forward slightly, eyes looking at the sword blade. Calm your heart and let the Chi sink down.

60. Finish - Return to Beginning Posture

Meaning of Classical Name:

When starting Tai Chi Sword, the sword was moved from the left hand to the right hand. Now, to finish, the right hand should place the sword back into the left hand. This also means to go back to the original position.

Common Name:

Receive the sword back into the original position.
The right hand gives the sword back to the left, returning to the beginning.

Description of Movement:

Drop the sword tip out and down while stepping back with the left foot. Expose the sword handle and take it into the left hand while stepping back with the right foot. Bring back the sword attached to the back of the left arm, right hand circles down to the right side and left leg is drawn back beside the right in the original preparation posture. This completes the Tai Chi sword form. Calm your heart and sink the Chi down to the Dan Tien.

Chapter 19

Order and Names of Each Posture of the Startling Rainbow Sword

1.) Look With Caution in All Directions (Preparation)
2.) Sleeping Tiger Awakes and Steps Forward
3.) Shen-zua Tsu-ru Pointing the Way (Immortal Points the Way)[1]
4.) Blending Yin and Yang
5.) Emperor Kills Giant Snake
6.) Coiled Dragon Bursts Upward
7.) Pin in Sleeve
8.) Dragon Coils and Stabs the Tiger
9.) Darting Bird Spins Its Body
10.) Shooting Star Orbits the Moon
11.) Spin Body, Stab Upwards
12.) Block Overhead
13.) Climb the Mountain, Chase Away the Moon
14.) Standing Incense
15.) Retreating and Blocking (Part 1)
16.) Retreating and Blocking (Part 2)
17.) Turn the Body and Attack the Lower Extremities
18.) Black Tiger Steals Spirit/Heart
19.) Tzashen-Kwan Raises His Weapons[2]
20.) Stealthful Wolf Turns Body
21.) Lowering Body, Sword Appears
22.) Wind Clears the Leaves
23.) Playing the Flute
24.) Carrying the Goods
25.) Bird Flies and Plunges Into the Waterfall, Then Embraces the Moon
26.) Spin and Attack
27.) Tai Kung Fishing (c)
28.) Wind Fills the Sails
29.) Pleasant Autumn Moon
30.) Black Tiger Retracts Claw
31.) Pushing Out the Boat

---

[1] Shen-zua Tsu-ru was a demigod, half man half god.
[2] Tzashen-Kwan was a warrior whose weapons were the Sun/Moon Rings.

32.) Child Praying
33.) Weaving Cloth
34.) Finch Diving (Part 1)
35.) Finch Diving (Part 2)
36.) Change Direction, Catch the Tiger
37.) Dragon Flies, Fung Hwong Bird Dances (Part 1) (d)
38.) Dragon Flies, Fung Hwong Bird Dances (Part 2)
39.) Golden Dragon Embraces the Pillar
40.) Eagle Snatches Prey
41.) Famous Champion's Statue
42.) Striking a Fish Under the Sea
43.) Unicorn Glances Behind at the Moon
44.) Repeat Strike Three Times
45.) Demon Measures the Sea
46.) Giant Snake Turns Over Its Body (Part 1)
47.) Giant Snake Turns Over Its Body (Part 2)
48.) Climb the Mountain, Chase Away the Moon
49.) Shin Flowers Fall in Autumn Rain
50.) Flying Dragon Startles the Rainbow
51.) Finish - Return to Beginning Posture

Origin of the Startling Rainbow Sword

Master Yin's army was in Southern China and it was in that particular area that a Martial Artist by the name of Too San Soon lived. He was a big man, intelligent and great conversationalist, therefore Master sought him out. It was to Master Yin's disappointment that Too San Soon was addicted to opium which causes one to become very lethargic, decreasing activity. Master Soon was obese and ceased to practice Kung-fu by the time Master Yin visited.

However, on this visit Master Yin learned of a family weapon which was carried by many generations of the men of this family. Master Soon's father and his father before him were all great Martial artists to have carried such a weapon. On this particular visit Master Yin saw the sword of Master Soon's ancestors hanging on the wall. Upon unsheathing the sword he saw it was rusted and not used for years which saddened Master Yin. Faded and barely legible was the name of the blade and which this form is named: Startling Rainbow.

[After the communist takeover of Mainland China, Master Yin relocated to Taiwan and began to rebuild his life. He continued his practice of Kung Fu and decided that if he developed a spectacular Sword form and named it The Startling Rainbow Sword that he might return some of the lost luster of the famous sword he had viewed in China.]

Chapter 20

Startling Rainbow Sword

(Name of Positions, Description of Movement and Positional Figures)*

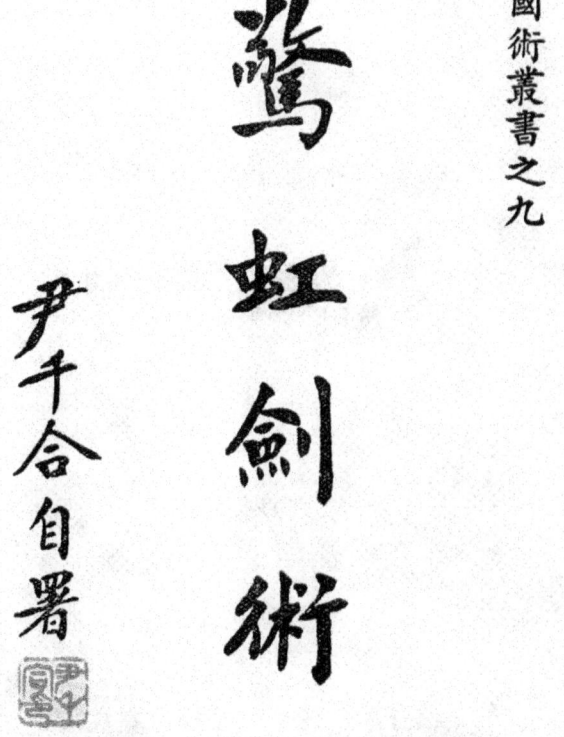

---

* The contemporary photographs, featuring Jeffery Lee Nickel, were taken from various angles that allowed the photographer to capture all aspects of the posture. These photographs have been labeled to avoid any confusion in direction. In addition, these photographs represent the evolution of the forms over several decades.

1. *Look With Caution in All Directions (Preparation)*

Description of Movement:

Eyes straight, sink chi to lower Dan Tien. Hold sword in left backhanded position, secret sword right hand.

2. *Sleeping Tiger Awakes and Steps Forward*

Description of Movement:

Start with left leg, walk three steps, finish in left cat stance. Right hand in secret sword position.

3. *Immortal Points the Way*

STARTLING RAINBOW SWORD

Description of Movement:

Turn to left while executing a block with the sword in a clockwise movement and return the arm to the left side, right hand strikes out remaining in a secret sword position.

4. *Blending Yin and Yang*

STARTLING RAINBOW SWORD

Description of Movement:

Pull left leg back into cat stance and place sword into right hand. Top hand is yin, bottom hand yang.

5. *Emperor Kills Giant Snake*

STARTLING RAINBOW SWORD

Description of Movement:

Pick up left knee while sword draws a counterclockwise circle.

6. *Coiled Dragon Bursts Upward*

*Last introductory posture before fighting postures and sword techniques

STARTLING RAINBOW SWORD

Description of Movement:

Draw right arm up overhead and turn slightly to the left.

7. *Pin in Sleeve*

STARTLING RAINBOW SWORD

Description of Movement:

In a circular movement, bring the sword down and around resting the body of the sword across the chest, prepare to attack.

8. *Dragon Coils and Stabs the Tiger*

STARTLING RAINBOW SWORD

Description of Movement:

Jump into a right cross-legged sitting stance. Sword stabs out at a downward angle piercing the enemy's leg.

9. *Darting Bird Spins Its Body*

STARTLING RAINBOW SWORD

Description of Movement:

Stand, pivot to your left full turn, blocking and striking.

10. *Shooting Star Orbits the Moon*

STARTLING RAINBOW SWORD

Description of Movement:

Block in front of body with sword in a clockwise circle, right leg steps forward and the left follows, stepping behind the right leg into a right cross legged sitting posture. As the blade spins and blocks the enemy has no opening to attack. Light reflecting off the blade resembles stars shooting through the sky.

11. *Spin Body, Stab Upwards*

STARTLING RAINBOW SWORD

Description of Movement:

Draw a counterclockwise circle with the sword. As the enemy attacks from behind, you spin and rise, stabbing the enemy in the face.

12. *Block Overhead*

Description of Movement:

Defend against a long weapon attack to head by blocking with sword as it redirects attack over your head.

13. *Climb the Mountain, Chase Away the Moon*

STARTLING RAINBOW SWORD

Description of Movement:

Step out with left foot staying low. Quickly transfer weight into left leg drawing the sword tip up and stab into the enemy's face.

14. *Standing Incense*

STARTLING RAINBOW SWORD

* Photographed From Different Angle

Description of Movement:

Block down and cut the enemy countering a low attack.

15. *Retreating and Blocking (Part 1)*

Description of Movement:

As a long weapon attacks high, you bring the body of the blade up in front of the body, blocking and redirecting the attack over your head. Repeat three times.

16. *Retreating and Blocking (Part 2)*

Description of Movement:

Picture illustrates the low point of interception during the execution of the movement.

17. *Turn the Body and Attack the Lower Extremities*

STARTLING RAINBOW SWORD

* Photographed From Different Angle

Description of Movement:

After the retreat, turn suddenly to the right and attack the enemy that approaches from behind.

18. *Black Tiger Steals Spirit/Heart*

Description of Movement:

As the enemy attacks from behind, you spin and stab him through the heart.

19. *Tzashen-Kwan Raises His Weapons*

STARTLING RAINBOW SWORD

Description of Movement:

Sword moves in a counterclockwise circle until it reaches the position shown. At the same time the right knee is lifted and the eyes look to the right. This is an on-guard position.

20. *Stealthful Wolf Turns Body*

* Photographed From Different Angle

Description of Movement:

Turn suddenly and strike down across the enemy's face.

21. *Lowering Body, Sword Appears*

Description of Movement:

Avoid a strike by going low as you attack the enemy's throat and face. This movement resembles the shape of a rainbow.

22. *Wind Clears the Leaves*

Description of Movement:

Stand up in a semi-squat while striking down with the sword, and then sweep the blade around your body to clear away enemies that surround you.

23. *Playing the Flute*

Description of Movement:

Previous movement cleared away your enemies, now survey the situation. Draw the sword back as shown and pick up your right leg.

24. *Carrying the Goods*

STARTLING RAINBOW SWORD

Description of Movement:

In the past, peasants carried goods to the market by hanging them from a pole across their shoulders. Step to the right and thrust out the sword while picking up the left knee. Next, look to the left and thrust out the secret sword hand as shown.

25. *Bird Flies and Plunges Into the Waterfall, Then Embraces the Moon*

STARTLING RAINBOW SWORD

Description of Movement:

Jumping inside crescent kick with a quarter turn, land in position shown.

26. *Spin and Attack*

Description of Movement:

Turn 135 degrees to your right, attack with a downward slash.

27. *Tai Kung Fishing*

* Photographed From Different Angle

Description of Movement:

Famous story of Tai Kung, he would hold his bait above the water and fish would jump into the air to take it. Blade makes a clockwise circle finishing with the right hand facing outward and in a right cat stance.

28. Wind Fills the Sails

STARTLING RAINBOW SWORD

* Photographed From Different Angle

Description of Movement:

First assume "Snake killing posture" (posture #5). Then, leap into the air to chase the enemy, land in a left mountain climbing stance and strike the enemy in the face.

29. *Pleasant Autumn Moon*

STARTLING RAINBOW SWORD

* Photographed From Different Angle

Description of Movement:

Circle the sword counterclockwise above head, right foot steps behind as the enemy attacks, turn and slash across their body.

30. *Black Tiger Retracts Claw*

Description of Movement:

Block with sword in a clockwise direction, then strike outward.

31. *Pushing Out the Boat*

Description of Movement:

Block as the enemy thrusts at your abdomen. Next, assume "Stealthful Wolf Turns Body," posture #20 (shown above).

32. *Child Praying*

STARTLING RAINBOW SWORD

Description of Movement:

Retreat to avoid strikes to lower body blocking with the sword and ending in posture shown.

33. *Weaving Cloth*

STARTLING RAINBOW SWORD

Description of Movement:

As you advance, the sword and secret sword hand move back and forth, finish in the posture "Carrying the Goods," posture #24 (shown above).

34. *Finch Diving (Part 1)*

Description of Movement:

As you fake retreat, block with the sword behind you. The picture illustrates the first posture.

35. *Finch Diving (Part 2)*

Description of Movement:

This illustration shows the second posture of this retreat technique. Repeat for a total of seven steps.

36. Change Direction, Catch the Tiger

*** Photographed From Different Angle**

Description of Movement:

After faking retreat, pivot on left foot, catching the enemy unprepared, and attack the least protected area. Land in a descending posture as shown.

37. Dragon Flies, Fung Hwong Bird Dances (Part 1)

*** Photographed From Different Angle**

Description of Movement:

Block the enemy's blade and strike their chest. For the Chinese, this title would conjure up strong images. The Dragon is male and flies proudly; the Fung Hwang bird is female and appears to be dancing. These postures appear in parts 1 and 2.

38. *Dragon Flies, Fung Hwong Bird Dances (Part 2)*

STARTLING RAINBOW SWORD

* Photographed From Different Angle

Description of Movement:

See previous posture.

39. *Golden Dragon Embraces the Pillar*

Description of Movement:

Turn around to the right and strike downward. Pick up right leg and draw in the sword as shown. Raised hand is the dragon's tail as the raised leg appears to be wrapped around a pillar. This is a transitional posture.

40. *Eagle Snatches Prey*

Description of Movement:

Like an eagle diving down on its prey you spin to the right and jump, landing in a cross legged sitting posture. The sword follows the movement of the body and cuts the enemy's legs. Repeat three times.

41. *Famous Champion's Statue*

STARTLING RAINBOW SWORD

Description of Movement:

In a circular movement, raise the sword above the head to block an attack.

42. *Striking a Fish Under the Sea*

STARTLING RAINBOW SWORD

*Photographed From Different Angle

Description of Movement:

After blocking overhead return to "Pin in Sleeve" (posture #7). Next, step out with the right leg to the rear angle and pick up left knee as you strike at the feet of the enemy.

43. *Unicorn Glances Behind at the Moon*

STARTLING RAINBOW SWORD

Description of Movement:

As the enemy attacks your chest, you pull back and target the forearm. From previous posture, pull the sword back placing it above the head while grabbing the left foot and raising it above the head. Next, step to the left with the left leg to achieve posture shown above.

44. Repeat Strike Three Times

STARTLING RAINBOW SWORD

* Photographed From Different Angle

Description of Movement:

First turn to the right and take the posture "Stealthful Wolf Turns Body," (posture #20). Then, retract into "golden dragon embraces pillar" (posture #39). Follow this with a step behind and spin, blocking and striking three times.

45. *Demon Measures the Sea*

STARTLING RAINBOW SWORD

Description of Movement:

First take the posture "embrace the moon" (posture #25). Then step out and strike the enemy's leg.

46. *Giant Snake Turns Over Its Body (Part 1)*

* Photographed From Different Angle

Description of Movement:

Counterclockwise circle movement of the sword followed by picking up left leg in front of body. This will block the enemy's attack.

47. *Giant Snake Turns Over Its Body (Part 2)*

Photographed From Different Angle

Description of Movement:

Pivot to the right and finish in a horse riding stance.

48. *Climb the Mountain, Chase Away the Moon*

STARTLING RAINBOW SWORD

*** Photographed From Different Angle**

Description of Movement:

Similar to posture #13. Withdraw into a cat stance. Run, jump, kick and step out with a thrust through your enemy. This is "fish jumps the watergate."

49. *Shin Flowers Fall in Autumn Rain*

STARTLING RAINBOW SWORD

Description of Movement:

First turn to the left (you now are facing in the same direction that you began the form). The body moves from center to the right, now to the left, and then returns to center. The movement resembles the petals of Chinese flowers falling to the ground, as if the autumn rain had struck them.

50. *Flying Dragon Startles the Rainbow*

STARTLING RAINBOW SWORD

* Photographed From Different Angle

Description of Movement:

Tossing the sword in the air resembles a flying dragon that startles the rainbow, causing it to disappear.

51. *Finish - Return to Beginning Posture*

Description of Movement:

Catch the sword in the left hand as you step back. Step back, left, right and together. You have now returned to the opening posture.